blue
rider
press

IN SEASON

BLUE RIDER PRESS | A MEMBER OF PENGUIN GROUP (USA) INC. | NEW YORK

IN SEASON

MORE THAN 150 FRESH AND SIMPLE RECIPES
FROM *NEW YORK* MAGAZINE INSPIRED BY
FARMERS' MARKET INGREDIENTS

ROB PATRONITE *and* ROBIN RAISFELD

New York FOOD EDITORS

blue
rider
press

Published by the Penguin Group
Penguin Group (USA) Inc., 375 Hudson Street, New York, New York 10014, USA •
Penguin Group (Canada), 90 Eglinton Avenue East, Suite 700, Toronto, Ontario M4P 2Y3, Canada
(a division of Pearson Penguin Canada Inc.) • Penguin Books Ltd, 80 Strand, London WC2R 0RL, England •
Penguin Ireland, 25 St Stephen's Green, Dublin 2, Ireland (a division of Penguin Books Ltd) •
Penguin Group (Australia), 707 Collins Street, Melbourne, Victoria 3008, Australia
(a division of Pearson Australia Group Pty Ltd) • Penguin Books India Pvt Ltd, 11 Community Centre,
Panchsheel Park, New Delhi–110 017, India • Penguin Group (NZ), 67 Apollo Drive, Rosedale,
Auckland 0632, New Zealand (a division of Pearson New Zealand Ltd) • Penguin Books,
Rosebank Office Park, 181 Jan Smuts Avenue, Parktown North 2193, South Africa • Penguin China,
B7 Jaiming Center, 27 East Third Ring Road North, Chaoyang District, Beijing 100020, China

Penguin Books Ltd, Registered Offices: 80 Strand, London WC2R 0RL, England

ISBN 978-0-399-16110-0

Printed in the United States of America
1   3   5   7   9   10   8   6   4   2

This book is printed on acid-free paper. ♾

Book design by Meighan Cavanaugh

The recipes contained in this book have been created for the ingredients and techniques indicated.
The publisher is not responsible for your specific health or allergy needs that may require supervision.
Nor is the publisher responsible for any adverse reactions you may have to the recipes contained in the book,
whether you follow them as written or modify them to suit your personal dietary needs or tastes.

While the authors have made every effort to provide accurate telephone numbers, Internet addresses, and other
contact information at the time of publication, neither the publisher nor the authors assume any responsibility
for errors, or for changes that occur after publication. Further, the publisher does not have any control
over and does not assume any responsibility for author or third-party websites or their content.

To our families

CONTENTS

SPRING

Asparagus • Burdock • Duck Eggs • Fiddlehead Ferns • Maple Syrup • Green Almonds • Green Garlic • New-Catch Holland Herring • Goat's-Milk Cheese • Mâche • Leeks • Lovage • Mangoes • Morels • Pea Shoots • Pheasant Eggs • Pineapple • Ramps • Rhubarb • Sheep's-Milk Ricotta • Scallions • Soft-Shell Crabs • Sorrel • Spinach • Bluefish • Broccoli Rabe • Coconut Macaroons • Dandelion Greens • Eggs • Stinging Nettles • Strawberries • White Asparagus

SUMMER

Black Mint • Fava Beans • Summer Flounder • Hardneck Garlic • Hatch Chile Peppers • Heirloom Tomatoes • "Regular" Tomatoes • Kirby Cucumbers • Santa Rosa Plums • Spearmint • Nasturtiums • Panisse Lettuce • Parsley • Peaches • *Pimientos de Padrón* • Purple Eggplant • Thai Chiles • Romaine Lettuce • Romano Beans • Squash Blossoms • Sugar Snap Peas • Local Artichokes • Avocado Squash • Breakfast Radishes • Basil • Bell Peppers • Cherries • Corn • Wild Blueberries • Sun Gold Tomatoes • Tomatillos • Sweet Potato Leaves • Turkish Orange Eggplant • Watermelon • Wild Alaskan King Salmon • Zucchini

INTRODUCTION

In 2004 *New York* magazine launched a weekly column called "In Season." Its goal was to spotlight a single ingredient, in most cases grown in the city's suburbs or exurbs and trucked in to Greenmarket, New York's pioneering network of farmers' markets, by the same person who'd harvested it days or sometimes hours before. Practical information came alongside the beauty shot in the form of a short, simple recipe contributed by a local chef and intended for the home cook. For anyone harboring an interest in eating locally and seasonally, the column strove to answer this perennial question: What's good right now, and what do I do with it?

Organized by season, these roughly 150 recipes do more than offer some of the country's top chefs' tips and techniques. Taken together, they chronicle how a year unfolds through food, and how truly seasonal eating depends more on the weather than on the calendar. They demonstrate how very little need be done with a fresh, seasonal ingredient at its peak—a happy consequence of the space constraints of the column, which is why most recipes showcase the featured ingredient in the simplest of preparations, as a salad, a pasta, a sandwich, a dessert, or even a condiment, meant to enhance a meal by rooting it in its seasonal context. They suggest how seasons overlap, and how, to anticipate and extend them, farmers outmaneuver Mother Nature with hoop houses, or high tunnels, greenhouses that give us greens all winter long, and "spring" crops overwintered from the previous fall, either in the ground or in storage.

The boom in farmers' markets and community-supported agriculture programs (CSAs) across the country signals a real desire to support local and regional agriculture, to eat sustainably and with the seasons. The incentives are obvious: ramps and fiddlehead ferns that herald the start of spring; fragrant Tristar strawberries too ripe and delicate for transport; lumpen heirloom tomatoes heavy with juice; frost-sweetened winter greens that sparkle with freshness. Ultimately, it's a hunger for flavor and variety that fuels what has become known as the locavore movement. But the term "locavore" might be misleading. *In Season* also celebrates seasonal ingredients from farther afield, ephemeral national treasures like wild Alaskan king salmon, Hatch green chiles from New Mexico, sweet Maine shrimp, and California Kishu mandarins, the kind of geographically specific raw materials that can transform a menu and anchor a meal.

In Season functions best, we hope, as a tool to navigate the increasingly diverse farmers' market and demystify less familiar ingredients, from crosnes to kohlrabi. But at its heart, it's a grateful acknowledgment of those growers and producers who feed our appetite for seasonal produce, and a vehicle for conveying the passion and creativity of the chefs who showcase it. Four of them—Gramercy Tavern's Michael Anthony, Babbo's Mario Batali, Momofuku's David Chang, and Annisa's Anita Lo—grace these pages with their personal thoughts on what it means to cook in season. We encourage you to join them.

THE *IN SEASON* PANTRY
AND RESOURCES

A quick guide to some things you'll want to have on hand, from the everyday to the exotic, and where to find them:

Lemons

For that crucial hit of acidity and brightness. Look for fruit that are heavy for their size with smooth, thin skin, and buy them often.

Garlic

The most essential aromatic. Although it stores well, it won't last forever, so keep replenishing your stock.

Salt and Pepper

Chefs can be extremely finicky about what kind of salt they prefer, but most agree that the use of high-quality sea salt improves the flavor of food and that proper seasoning is what distinguishes a confident professional from a timid amateur. You'll want a high-quality coarse-grained sea salt such as Maldon or a fine French fleur de sel for finishing, and a good kosher salt for more basic tasks. Where pepper is called for, always grind it fresh.

Extra-Virgin Olive Oil

A perfectly ripe August tomato is a beautiful thing. To drizzle it with subpar olive oil does it no favors. That's why when you ask chefs what they can't live without, nearly every time, they answer "really good olive oil." Using the high-quality extra-virgin variety will infinitely improve everything with which it comes in contact—pasta, salads, soups, beans, bruschetta, raw and cooked vegetables. Your dinner guests will think you're a genius. *Extra-virgin*, by the way, refers to oils made from the first pressing of the olives. Flavorwise, this oil is naturally superior to the stuff that follows in the production cycle, including oil made from the remains of the first pressing and classified as *virgin*. Lower down on the totem pole is plain old *olive oil* (aka *pure*). Incidentally, olives are as seasonal as any other fruit (see New-Harvest Olive Oil, page 77). Once they're picked in the fall, they begin to lose their flavor and character; thus, it's crucial to press them immediately. Among the most highly prized olive oils are the exceptionally vibrant, peppery ones made from just-ripe-enough olives at the beginning of the season, usually in November. Like wines, olive oils vary tremendously depending on terroir, weather, vintage, at what stage of ripeness the olives were pressed, and how the oil was produced. So, just as you might not want to restrict your wine consumption to, say, one particular California Chardonnay, it's nice to have some variety in your olive-oil life. We typically try to have several on hand, from a big-flavored, unfiltered, estate-bottled Tuscan to the comparatively budget-friendly Olave from Chile. Try to buy yours from a shop that lets you sample the oils, and take full advantage of that policy.

Cheese

The only three cheeses you need to know (at least for the purposes of this book): Parmigiano-Reggiano (the aged, granular cow's-milk cheese made in Emilia-Romagna or Lombardy), *grana padano* (typically younger, milder, and less expensive), and pecorino Toscano (a sheep's-milk alternative). They're all Italian, and they're all shaved, grated, or dusted with semi-abandon within these pages.

Bread

There are several recipes in this book for variously topped bruschetta, and good bruschetta begins with good bread. We like to use a dark-and-crackly-crusted Italian variety with a nice springy crumb like the *truccione saré* from Sullivan St Bakery in New York City. But any rustic country loaf will do. Toasting the bread in the oven, in a toaster, or on a grill, then rubbing it with garlic and drizzling it with olive oil works fine. Griddling, though, is our favorite method: Cut the bread into half-inch slices. Pour two tablespoons of extra-virgin olive oil in a nonstick pan over medium heat. Put the slices in the pan and rub them around a little to absorb the oil. Flip the bread over and cook, under a weight if necessary, until it's golden brown but still tender. Flip it again and cook the other side.

Dried Pasta

You want the kind that tastes good enough to eat by itself, unsauced. Well, maybe with a little butter and Parmesan. The best is made from semolina, coarsely ground durum wheat. It's superior in flavor to every other type, and results in a nice firm noodle. Look for pasta that appears rough on the surface (as opposed to smooth and glossy). That indicates it was probably extruded through bronze dies, which best creates the desired sauce-gripping texture. It's also a sign that it was probably dried slowly and carefully at low temperatures (sometimes for days), which helps retain the grain's wheaty essence. Our favorite brands, in no particular order, include Afeltra (available at the Manhattan branch of the Turin-based megamarket Eataly); Benedetto Cavalieri; Rustichella; Latini; and Setaro, which comes in lovely, unusual shapes like *calamarata*, *maccheroncini*, *paccheri*, and *nodi marini* (sailor's knots, available at buonitalia.com). Because of the time and labor involved in making these pastas, they don't come cheap. That said, we once conducted a blind spaghetti taste test with a few of New York's top Italian chefs, and the 99-cent-per-pound Trader Joe's brand scored a big upset victory over some major pasta players.

Colatura, Anchovies, and Bottarga

Italian might very well be our national cuisine—or close to it—but some ingredients used in these pages are still relatively unknown, or at least unloved: *colatura*, the cured anchovy sauce that imparts a deep, umami-rich flavor; *bottarga di muggine*, gray mullet roe that's pressed into a shavable block; and salt-packed anchovies, the secret trick up many a Mediterranean-inspired chef's sleeve. New York is blessed with some excellent Italian grocers, some of whom ply their wares online.

Chefs especially love these two: dipaloselects.com, affably overseen by cheese maven Lou Di Palo, and buonitalia.com, where restaurateur Tony May's brother, Mimmo, runs the show.

Spanish Ingredients

Spanish ingredients have become much more accessible with the rise of tapas bars and the influence of megachefs like José Andrés and Ferran Adrià. If you can't locate essentials like *pimentón* (Spanish smoked paprika) or *mojama* (salt-cured tuna loin), try despanabrandfoods.com, the online retail arm of an excellent importer based in Queens, New York.

Asian Ingredients

With Sriracha nearly as common on restaurant tables in New York as ketchup, Asian flavors continue to captivate chefs and eaters of all culinary stripes, and you'll note many recipes call for ingredients such as Japanese-made Kewpie mayonnaise, mirin (rice wine), the Thai fish sauce *nam pla*, Thailand's Golden Mountain sauce (made from fermented soybeans), and *gochujang* (the Korean hot pepper paste). Asian groceries are proliferating around the country, and in New York, we've had good luck at Sunrise Mart, Asia Market, and Bangkok Center Grocery. A chain of Korean markets called Han Ah Reum also offers its products online at hmart.com.

Bacon

If you have trouble finding a great locally smoked bacon, try these top-notch purveyors: bentons countryhams2.com, nueskes.com, and smokehouse.com (the online home of Burgers' sliced country jowl, featured in Tien Ho's BLT, page 168).

Specialists and Generalists

When it comes to obscure spices, oils, and sauces, it's nearly impossible to stump Kalustyan's, the ambrosial epicenter of all things Middle Eastern, South Asian, and more. If you can't find mustard oil and wasabi oil in your area, you will at kalustyans.com.

Another favorite online bazaar, zingermans.com, provides easy access to the famed Ann Arbor deli's carefully curated inventory of cured meats, cheeses, oils, vinegars, sauces, and condiments.

Local Produce, Wherever You Live

The website localharvest.org is a terrific reference for farmers' markets and community-supported agriculture programs around the country, while justfood.org focuses on the five boroughs of New York City. Information about New York City Greenmarket locations, schedules, and participating farmers can be found at grownyc.org/greenmarket.

As a cook, I feel anticipation and rebirth through spring and exuberant celebration in summer, but my favorite season, autumn, brings on a contemplative reverence.

Fall continues what the heat of summer put in motion: the explosion of peppers, tomatoes, eggplant, corn, beans, berries, cucumbers. The Harvest! There is balance in the air. The intensity of the sun fades and provides those perfectly long days that begin and end in coolness. We cook with a feeling of abundance.

As fall progresses, the moon grows bright and we get a glimpse of sadness, a need for comfort, an uncertainty in the air, a warning that this won't last forever. One last bite that might be the best of the year since we know it will be another twelve months until we can taste that flavor again.

Plants slow down their growth and the days get shorter through this transition. Mud replaces dust. This triggers an innate reaction in plants and cooks to store things—pickled, salted, smoked, and preserved. We turn to foods that are beautifully sun drenched with golds, oranges, and crimsons and are protected by heavy skins and earth. Pumpkins of all sizes, associated with demons, hide in the fields. Apples and pears weigh down tree branches; some varieties have been here for ages while others have come from the belief that "creativity means not copying."

In this season, as soon as I feel the first cool winds and smell a little smoke in the air, something triggers my sense of home and I find myself searching for a fire. At last, Gramercy Tavern brings me to hearth and home.

—MICHAEL ANTHONY, EXECUTIVE CHEF/PARTNER, GRAMERCY TAVERN

FALL

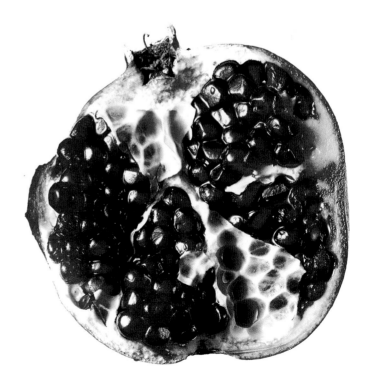

ASIAN PEARS

There are more than a hundred varieties of this mildly sweet and juicy fruit available in Japan. So it's odd that in the United States, where you can find at least a couple dozen, they're rarely categorized by their individual names. Nevertheless, they all share a spectacular crunchiness, which makes them ideal for seasonal salads like the one below from Iron Chef Masaharu Morimoto.

Masaharu Morimoto's Asian Pear Salad

1 large Asian pear

Juice of 1 lemon

1 cup plum wine

2 tablespoons white balsamic vinegar

1 shallot, finely minced

6 ounces olive oil

Salt and freshly ground white pepper
    to taste

4 bunches mâche, washed

1 tablespoon fresh chives, cut into
    ½-inch pieces

2 tablespoons coarsely chopped,
    toasted hazelnuts

Cut the Asian pear into julienne strips. Place in cold water with the lemon juice and reserve.

FOR THE VINAIGRETTE: In a saucepan, bring plum wine to a simmer and reduce to ¼ cup. In a small bowl, combine the wine with the vinegar and shallot. Slowly drizzle in the oil, whisking to emulsify. Season to taste with the salt and white pepper.

To plate, toss the julienned Asian pear with the mâche, chives, and enough vinaigrette to coat. Adjust seasoning. Place in the center of a plate, drizzle with remaining vinaigrette, and sprinkle with toasted hazelnuts. *Serves 4.*

ALBACORE TUNA

After a summer spent feasting on sardines, assorted crustaceans, and the occasional squid, North Atlantic albacore tuna, *Thunnus alalunga*, are at their peak. Their pink flesh is the palest in color and mildest in flavor of all tuna varieties, but also among the fattiest, and takes well to this Japanese blackened-tuna-sandwich treatment that Andrew Carmellini gives the fish at The Dutch.

Andrew Carmellini's Tuna Kuroyaki Sandwich

FOR THE *YUZU* DRESSING

2 teaspoons sugar

3 tablespoons rice vinegar

¼ cup *yuzu* juice (see Note)

⅓ cup grapeseed oil

½ red Thai chile, finely diced

FOR THE *TOBIKO* MAYO

¼ cup Hellmann's mayonnaise

½ cup Kewpie mayonnaise

3 scallions, sliced thin

1 teaspoon *yuzu kosho* (see Note)

1 tablespoon fresh lime juice

⅛ teaspoon salt

2 tablespoons *tobiko* (see Note)

FOR THE TUNA

1½ pounds albacore, cut into 4 portions, about 3½ inches wide and 1 inch thick

Salt and pepper to taste

¼ cup *togarashi* (see Note)

½ cup canola oil

FOR THE SANDWICH

4 soft rolls

1 (2.4-ounce) package *tenkasu* (tempura flakes) (see Note)

½ head iceberg lettuce, leaves separated

1 beefsteak tomato, sliced medium thin and seasoned with salt and pepper

½ cucumber, cut in half widthwise, sliced thin lengthwise, and soaked in *yuzu* dressing

Note: *Available in most Asian groceries.*

FOR THE *YUZU* DRESSING: Mix ingredients in a bowl and refrigerate overnight.

FOR THE *TOBIKO* MAYO: Mix ingredients together in a bowl and refrigerate.

FOR THE FISH: Season both sides of each piece of tuna with salt, pepper, and *togarashi*. Heat half the canola oil in a large pan over high heat. Sear the fish on both sides, 2 pieces at a time. Cook to medium-rare. Repeat with remaining pieces.

TO ASSEMBLE THE SANDWICH: Cut the rolls in half and lightly toast insides so they're crisp. Spread each side with *tobiko* mayo and sprinkle *tenkasu* over the mayo. Starting from the bottom, layer with 2 or 3 slices of lettuce, 1 slice of tomato, tuna, and 2 slices of cucumber. ***Serves 4.***

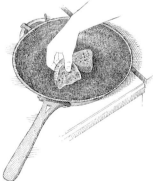
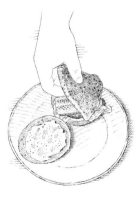

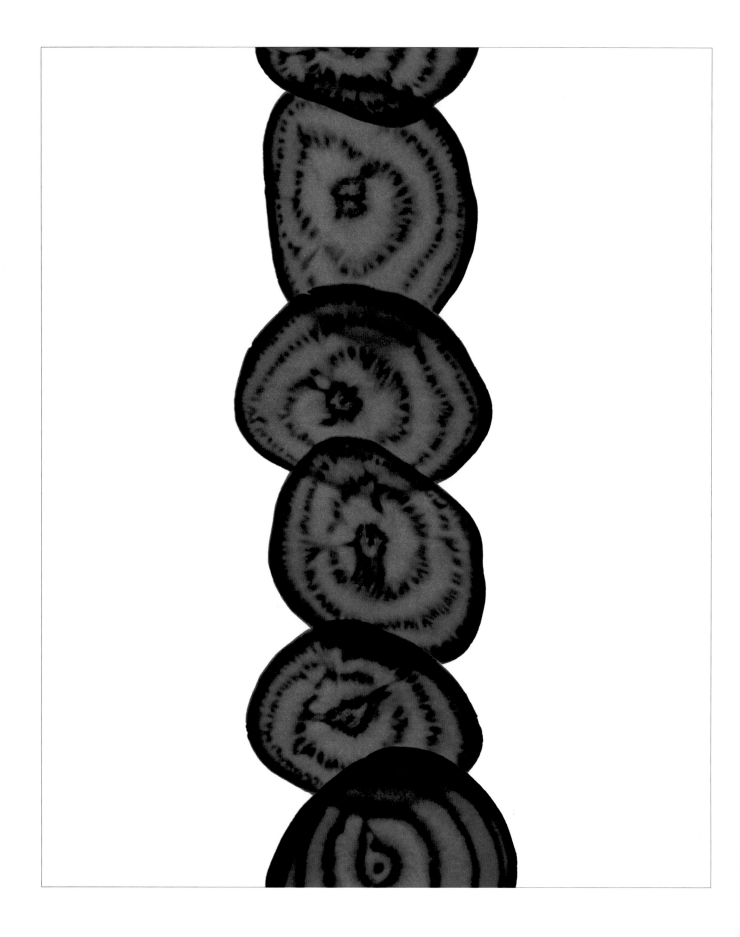

BEETS

The beet's distinctively sweet and earthy flavor profile is a familiar presence in soups and salads. It has yet, however, to make much headway in the modern world of mixed drinks. One notable exception is this root-vegetable riff on a Negroni, served at the retro-Italian diner Parm in New York's Nolita. Engineered by partner Jeff Zalaznick, the combination of beet-infused gin with herbaceous sweet vermouth and bitter Campari makes for a biting and botanical pink-and-purple twist on a classic cocktail.

Parm's Beet Negroni

2 to 3 large raw red beets

1 (750-ml.) bottle Bluecoat American
    dry gin

1 ounce Campari

1 ounce Carpano Antica sweet vermouth

Orange zest, for garnish

Dice beets. Soak in gin in a pitcher or jar for 48 hours. Using a funnel, strain through a coffee filter back into the gin bottle. Combine 1 ounce each of beet gin, Campari, and vermouth in a mixing glass. Add ice, and stir. Strain, and serve over ice with orange zest. ***Makes 1 drink.***

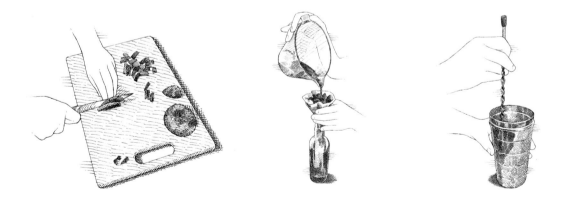

BINTJE POTATOES

The tiny, smooth-skinned, yellow-fleshed Bintje (pronounced *bin-tchuh*) was developed a century ago by a Dutch botanist-school-teacher who named it for a star pupil. Neither exceptionally starchy nor waxy, it's a remarkably flavorful French-fry-lover's potato. Connoisseurs of Belgian frites slice them thick, fry them twice, dip them in mayo, and accept no substitutes. Bintjes are also fluffy and delicious mashed, and even better mashed, then pan-fried—a technique chef Yvon de Tassigny uses at the newfangled Brooklyn steakhouse St. Anselm, which this recipe is adapted from.

Yvon de Tassigny's Pan-Fried Mashed Potatoes

2½ pounds Bintje potatoes, peeled

Pinch of fresh rosemary

1 scallion, chopped

½ teaspoon minced garlic

2 tablespoons extra-virgin olive oil

8 tablespoons (1 stick) unsalted butter

Salt and freshly ground black pepper to taste

1 tablespoon rendered bacon or duck fat

½ teaspoon white truffle oil (optional for white-truffle-oil haters)

Handful of chopped parsley

Cut the potatoes into even pieces or slices, and rinse under cold water. Boil potatoes in a pot of water until fork-tender, and drain. Return potatoes to the pot, and dry over low heat for a couple of minutes. Fold in the rosemary, scallion, garlic, olive oil, and butter; season with salt and pepper; and mash the potatoes, then let cool to room temperature. In an 8-inch pan, heat the bacon or duck fat. Add the mashed potatoes almost to the lip of the pan, and press down gently with your hand to form a pancake of sorts. Cook over medium-high heat until a crust forms on the bottom, about 5 to 10 minutes. Flip the potatoes in a pan or invert onto a plate and slide them back into the pan to cook the other side until a crust forms. Plate the potatoes, and sprinkle with truffle oil, if using, and parsley. ***Serves 4.***

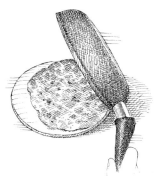

BRUSSELS SPROUTS

When you think about it, it's rather amazing how the once-humdrum (if not downright detested) Brussels sprout has shot to menu stardom. We've had them deep-fried, shaved raw, and countless other ways. But very few preparations can compare to the one we first encountered at Franny's in Brooklyn: roasted to ineluctable sweetness and combined with pecorino and good olive oil.

Andrew Feinberg's
Roasted Brussels Sprouts
with Walnuts and Pecorino

½ cup walnuts, crumbled

24 Brussels sprouts, halved

Extra-virgin olive oil

Salt and freshly ground
    black pepper

Lemon

Pecorino Toscano

Toast the walnuts on a baking sheet at 350 degrees for about 10 minutes, until golden brown; set aside. Turn oven temperature up to 450. Toss halved Brussels sprouts in a bowl with enough extra-virgin olive oil (2 to 3 tablespoons) to lightly coat each sprout. Season with salt and pepper. Lay sprouts on baking sheet and roast until fork-tender and some leaves have become crunchy (about 20 minutes). Let sprouts cool, then toss in a bowl with the walnuts. Drizzle liberally with olive oil, add a squeeze of lemon, and season with salt and pepper. Shave aged pecorino Toscano on top. *Serves 4.*

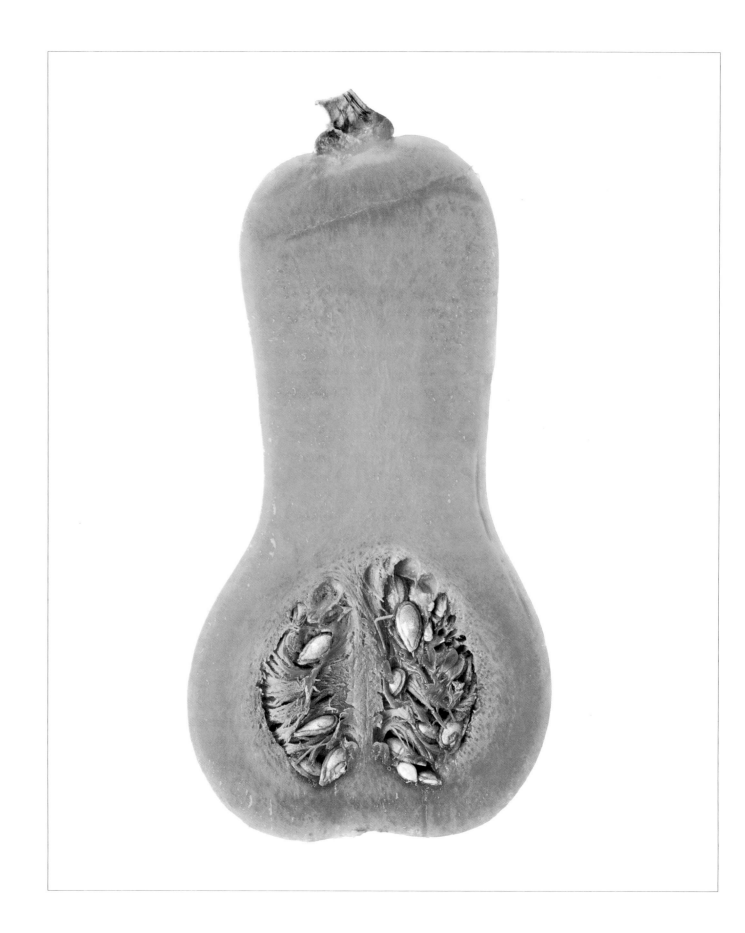

BUTTERNUT SQUASH

There is little you can't do with the multipurpose butternut: bake it, simmer it, steam it, or make soup. But 'Ino owner Jason Denton's butternut squash bruschetta just might be the niftiest use of a gourd since the jack-o'-lantern. Beneath the distinctive bell-shaped, beige-hued shell, the deeper orange the color, the sweeter the flesh.

'Ino's Butternut Squash Bruschetta

1 pound butternut squash (to yield
   2 cups)

2 tablespoons honey

½ teaspoon crushed red pepper flakes

10 caperberries, roughly chopped

10 walnuts, roughly chopped

2 tablespoons extra-virgin olive oil

½ teaspoon kosher salt

Pinch of freshly ground black pepper

1 baguette, cut on the bias into 12
   1½-inch-thick slices

2 tablespoons walnut oil

4 teaspoons grated asiago cheese

Preheat oven to 400 degrees. Peel and seed squash and cut into 1-inch cubes. In a medium bowl, gently toss the squash, honey, red pepper flakes, caperberries, walnuts, olive oil, salt, and black pepper. Spread mixture evenly on ungreased baking sheet. Bake 10 minutes, then gently stir ingredients, and continue to cook for another 15 minutes, until soft. Remove from oven and let cool to room temperature. Meanwhile, toast the baguette slices in the oven or press on a panini press until slightly crisp. Scoop a generous tablespoon of the squash mixture onto each piece of baguette. Adjust seasoning with salt and pepper and garnish with a drizzle of walnut oil and grated asiago. **Serves 6.**

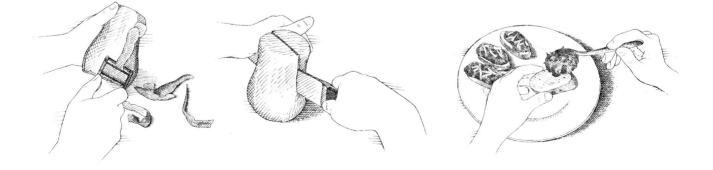

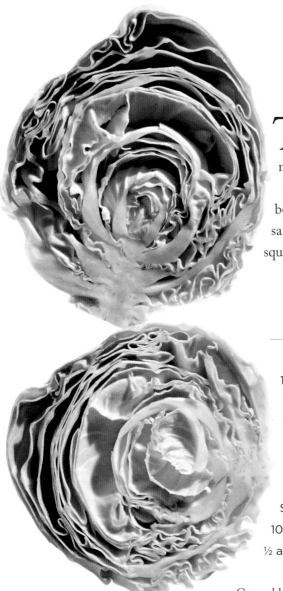

CABBAGE

The fall market teems with cabbage of all sorts: tiny compact heads, long-leaved Asian varieties, and those frilly oversize marvels, unfurled in O'Keeffe-ian splendor. Cooked, the plant makes a satisfying cold-weather food, but we might like it even better in Hecho en Dumbo chef Danny Mena's crunchy, piquant salad, given a south-of-the-border flavor profile with *queso fresco*, a squeeze of lime, and crumbled hibiscus flowers.

Danny Mena's Ensalada Rosaura

1 small or ½ large cabbage

½ red onion, sliced thin

¼ pound *queso fresco*

3 tablespoons Champagne vinegar

3 tablespoons extra-virgin olive oil, plus more for frying

Juice of 1 lime

Salt and freshly ground black pepper to taste

10 dried hibiscus flowers

½ avocado, sliced

Cut cabbage in quarters and remove the core. Slice the cabbage into thin shreds. In a large bowl, combine cabbage with sliced onion. Crumble the cheese over the salad and toss with Champagne vinegar, olive oil, and lime juice. Season with salt and pepper. Let stand for 2 to 3 hours or refrigerate overnight. When ready to serve, fry the hibiscus flowers in a little olive oil; allow to cool. Crumble fried hibiscus flowers over salad and garnish with sliced avocado. ***Serves 4.***

  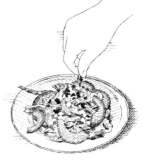

CIPOLLINI

Come fall, the hunger for the fresh and the raw is replaced by the desire to simmer and braise—two cooking methods that particularly suit cipollini, the onionlike bulbs of the grape hyacinth. The flying saucer–shaped Italian import has taken root here, and squat specimens can be found each fall at New York's Union Square Greenmarket—just a short hop away from Union Square Cafe, the source of this sweet-and-sour recipe from chef Michael Romano.

Michael Romano's Glazed Cipollini

1 pound cipollini

2 tablespoons butter

½ teaspoon kosher salt

⅛ teaspoon freshly ground black pepper

2 cups red wine

2 tablespoons honey

1 bay leaf

Soak cipollini in ice water for an hour to make them easier to peel. Peel with a paring knife. Heat butter in a saucepan or straight-sided skillet over medium flame until it turns nutty brown. Add cipollini and cook, stirring, about 8 minutes, until golden brown. Season with salt and pepper. Add wine, honey, and bay leaf. Bring to a boil, reduce heat, and simmer uncovered for 20 to 25 minutes, until cipollini are tender. Raise heat and boil until wine has reduced and glazed the cipollini; stir often to coat and adjust heat as necessary to prevent glaze from sticking to the pan. Serve immediately, ideally as an accompaniment to any roasted meat. ***Serves 6.***

CONCORD GRAPES

Never underestimate the potential of the Concord grape, an intensely aromatic, quintessentially grapey East Coast variety that, for many, embodies autumn. Look what happened to poor Ephraim Bull, who introduced the Concord in the 1850s but died broke. While he was basking in the glow of his handiwork, others were thinking juice, jams, and PB&J. "He sowed, others reaped," reads his tombstone. This recipe for sweet but sophisticated Concord grape ketchup comes courtesy of Charleen Badman, who made her name working in Manhattan kitchens including Lobster Club and Inside, and currently practices her hyperseasonal, produce-centric style at FnB in her hometown of Scottsdale, Arizona. Try it with robust cheeses like Boerenkaas or mild-flavored roast fish like cod.

Charleen Badman's Concord Grape Ketchup

3 quarts Concord
   grapes, stemmed
½ cup water
¾ cup brown sugar
1 cup granulated sugar
1 cup apple cider
1½ teaspoons cinnamon

1 teaspoon salt
¾ teaspoon ground ginger
½ teaspoon ground allspice
¼ teaspoon ground clove
¼ teaspoon freshly
   ground black pepper

In a 4-quart saucepan, cook grapes and water over medium heat until the grapes release their juice. Strain juice and discard skins and seeds. Combine juice with remaining ingredients in a saucepot. Reduce over medium heat for 30 minutes. Let cool and serve. *Makes 3 cups.*

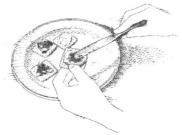

ESCAROLE

*L*ike its fellow members of the Cichorium family, radicchio and frisée, the loose-leafed escarole makes a terrific salad. But the plant, with its slightly bitter flavor and sturdy texture, also stands up well to cooking, which is what makes it a contorni staple at so many red-sauce joints. At the seasonally minded, subterranean beer bar Jimmy's No. 43 in New York's East Village, owner Jimmy Carbone eschews the simple garlic-sauté treatment for something a bit meatier: big slabs of bacon and a dressing made from the fat.

Jimmy Carbone's Wilted Escarole and Slab Bacon

2 slices slab bacon, cut ¼ inch thick (Carbone
    recommends Benton's, Nodine's, and Nueske's)
Extra-virgin olive oil (optional)
1 garlic clove, sliced
Calabrese red pepper flakes
1 cup escarole leaves, cleaned and trimmed
Half a lemon
Balsamic vinegar
Salt

Cook slab bacon in a hot cast-iron skillet on both sides until crisp but not hard. Remove from pan directly to salad bowl. Do not wipe bacon, as the fat and natural drippings will become the dressing. If there isn't sufficient bacon fat in the skillet to cook the escarole, add some extra-virgin olive oil. Briefly sauté the garlic, red pepper flakes, and escarole to quickly wilt the greens. Remove to the salad bowl and toss with the bacon. Dress the salad with a squeeze of lemon, a drizzle of balsamic vinegar, and salt to taste. *Serves 2.*

EAST COAST OYSTERS

Despite that persistent old wives' tale, it's okay to eat oysters year-round, even during months lacking an *r*. Something called refrigeration took care of that. Still, the very best time for slurping oysters is during the fall and winter, when the bivalves are especially sweet, crisp, and tender. There's nothing wrong with Pacific oysters, but it's generally agreed among connoisseurs that the ones from off the coast of Long Island and Cape Cod are culinarily superior. Gulped down straight from the craggy half-shell in great Diamond Jim Brady quantities, they're hard to beat. Slipping a few into a wok-cooked omelette, as Zak Pelaccio does at his Malaysian canteen, Fatty Crab, comes close.

Zak Pelaccio's Oyster Omelette

3 large eggs

1 tablespoon dark soy sauce

Pinch of salt

3 tablespoons peanut oil

3 small or medium-size Atlantic oysters, such as Blue Points, Wellfleets, or Widow's Holes, shucked and reserved in their liquor

Kecap manis (available at Asian grocery stores)

Sriracha sauce

2 scallions, chopped

2 sprigs cilantro, picked

Beat eggs in a medium bowl with soy sauce and pinch of salt. Place a wok over high heat until very hot. Add the peanut oil. When the oil begins to smoke, add the egg mixture and fry for about 30 to 45 seconds, tilting and shaking the wok to allow the uncooked egg in the center to cook evenly. Place oysters on top of omelette and flip (or turn it over with a spatula) and cook for a few more seconds. Slide omelette onto a paper-towel-lined plate to absorb the grease. Flip again onto a serving plate. Garnish with *kecap manis*, Sriracha, chopped scallions, and cilantro leaves. Serve immediately. ***Serves 1.***

HOW TO SHUCK AN OYSTER

First of all, you'll need a good oyster knife, a thickish towel or glove, and a firm resolve—like removing a compact disk from its plastic wrapper, oyster shucking takes practice.

Hold the oyster on one end, flat side up, so you don't lose any of its liquor. Insert oyster knife into the narrow hinge and twist firmly until the top shell releases and pops open.

Slide the oyster knife under the flat top shell, cutting through the muscle and detaching the shell.

Now slide the oyster knife along the inside of the bottom shell to loosen the oyster from its grip.

ROMANESCO

*I*magine a head of cauliflower as envisioned by Jerry Garcia and you have the Romanesco, a Day-Glo green, spiral-floreted variety that looks like the lead in a psychedelic version of *Little Shop of Horrors*. If only its season lasted a little longer, you could hang miniature Christmas ornaments on it. Even deconstructed and sautéed, though, it's equally striking in this recipe from Porsena's Sara Jenkins, who resorts to a few of her favorite tricks: toasted bread crumbs for crunch, anchovy for flavor, and pasta imported from Naples—but any good-quality variety will do.

Sara Jenkins's Maccheroncini *with Romanesco*

¼ cup bread crumbs

2 tablespoons extra-virgin olive oil

2 tablespoons butter

4 cups Romanesco florets

¼ cup pitted Gaeta olives

1 tablespoon capers, drained and rinsed

1 garlic clove, smashed

2 anchovy fillets

1 pound short dried tubular pasta, such as *maccheroncini*

Salt and freshly ground black pepper

In a large skillet, fry bread crumbs in 1 tablespoon olive oil over medium heat until golden brown and set aside. Melt butter with the remaining olive oil. Add the florets to the pan and brown over high heat. Add the olives, capers, garlic, and anchovies and sauté until slightly crisp, lightly stiring until anchovies are broken up. Meanwhile, cook the pasta per package directions. Drain, toss with sauce and bread crumbs, and add salt and pepper to taste. ***Serves 4.***

BOSC PEARS

Sweet and rich, with a fine-grained flesh that's firmer than most, the russet Bosc is a workhorse pear that's perfect for cooking. Like all pears, Boscs are mealy if picked ripe. It's best to buy immature specimens and ripen them in a paper bag. When the neck of the pear gives slightly under gentle pressure, it's ready to eat—or, better yet, to quickly sauté and then bake, as in this recipe from pear aficionado François Payard of François Payard Bakery.

François Payard's
Brown Butter Roasted Pears

4 nearly ripe Bosc pears (d'Anjou or very firm Bartletts are fine, too)

4 tablespoons unsalted butter, plus 2 tablespoons to finish sauce

¾ cup maple syrup

½ vanilla bean, scraped

Vanilla ice cream, for serving

Preheat oven to 375 degrees. Slice pears in half, leaving stem intact, and using a melon baller, core each half. Over medium-high heat, brown 4 tablespoons of the butter in a large ovenproof sauté pan. Add pear halves, cut side down, and sear for approximately 2 minutes, or until slightly caramelized. Add the maple syrup to the pan and bring to a boil. Scrape the vanilla-bean seeds into the pan and add the pod. Transfer the pan to the oven and roast for approximately 5 to 7 minutes, or until pears are slightly tender. Remove pear from pan. Strain the remaining sauce from the sauté pan into a saucepan and bring to a boil, stirring occasionally. Remove pan from stove and allow to cool for 5 minutes, then whisk in the remaining 2 tablespoons of butter. Plate each pear half individually, drizzle with sauce, and serve with vanilla ice cream. *Serves 8.*

BROCCOLI

Despite its undeniable elegance and utter deliciousness, broccoli is not a universally loved vegetable. Just ask any small child or forty-first president of the United States. For this, Craig Koketsu of the hyperseasonal restaurant Park Avenue has a somewhat shocking solution: crushing and then sprinkling Cheetos over the healthful crucifer. Now, as far as we know, Cheetos—whether they be of the original crunchy or the puffy baked variety—are not a seasonal food. But let's not quibble. "It's our most popular side dish," says Koketsu. "It outsells French fries."

Craig Koketsu's Broccoli and Cheetos

FOR THE BROCCOLI

3 large heads of broccoli, stems peeled and cut into ¼-inch disks; florets cut into small pieces

3 tablespoons extra-virgin olive oil

2 garlic cloves, finely chopped

1 teaspoon dried red pepper flakes

3 tablespoons butter

Salt to taste

FOR THE CHEESE SAUCE

1 quart heavy cream

2 tablespoons chopped shallot

2 tablespoons chopped garlic

10 black peppercorns

1 bay leaf

2 cups grated aged Gouda cheese

1 cup grated Parmesan cheese

Salt to taste

½ 9-ounce bag of Cheetos Puffs

FOR THE BROCCOLI: Blanch florets and stems in boiling salted water for 3 minutes. Remove and shock in ice water. Cool and drain. Place large sauté pan over medium-high heat. Add olive oil, garlic, and pepper flakes and sweat, being careful not to brown garlic. Add butter and melt fully into oil. When the butter and oil begin to bubble, add broccoli and sauté until heated through. Adjust seasoning with salt and reserve broccoli on a paper-towel-lined plate.

FOR THE CHEESE SAUCE: In a heavy-bottomed saucepan, reduce cream with shallot, garlic, peppercorns, and bay leaf until it thickly coats the back of a spoon. Remove from heat and whisk in cheeses until fully melted. Adjust seasoning with salt. Strain sauce through fine-mesh strainer and keep warm in a bain-marie. Crush the Cheetos in the bag into pebble-size bits with a rolling pin.

TO SERVE: Pour warm sauce into a large serving dish. Arrange broccoli on top of sauce. Top with crushed Cheetos. *Serves 6 to 8.*

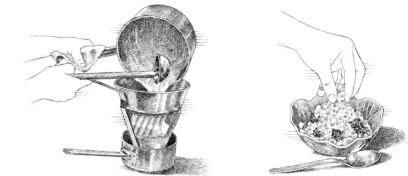

Another terrific approach to the emerald-green superfood takes its flavor cues not from the American snack-food shelf, but from southern Italy. That's the ancestral birthplace of *colatura* (essentially, cured anchovy drippings), the umami-rich secret to this superb salad from Brooklyn's locavore pizzeria Franny's.

Franny's Roasted-Broccoli Salad
with Colatura *and* Chiles

2 heads of broccoli

Extra-virgin olive oil

Salt and freshly ground black pepper to taste

½ cup water

Juice of 2 lemons

2 tablespoons *colatura*

1 tablespoon finely chopped Calabrian chiles

1 tablespoon minced garlic

¼ cup red onion batons

Preheat oven to 450 degrees. Cut away broccoli florets and any nice leaves from stem. Roughly chop leaves and reserve. Toss florets with a generous coating of olive oil, salt, and pepper, and spread evenly on a baking sheet or roasting pan. Pour ¼ cup of water over the broccoli, and roast in oven for 12 to 15 minutes. Remove broccoli from oven, and let cool completely. Warm a tablespoon of olive oil in a pan over medium heat, add broccoli leaves and remaining ¼ cup of water, and cook until leaves are tender. Remove and let cool completely. Mix lemon juice, *colatura*, chiles, and garlic in a serving bowl. Add onions, broccoli leaves, and florets; toss well. Drizzle in an additional teaspoon of olive oil. Serve cool in chilled bowls. ***Serves 4.***

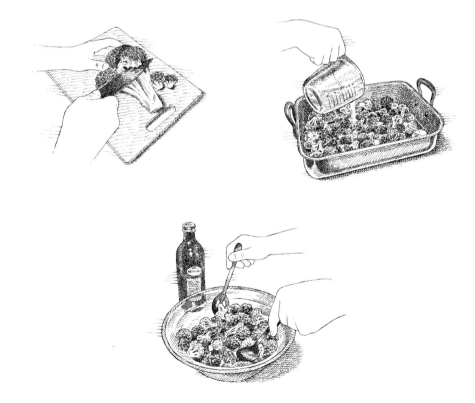

BROCCOLI SPIGARELLO

This heirloom broccoli rabe variety (some claim it's the granddaddy of all broccoli rabe) has a cult following in California, where Bret Macris, now the chef at Brooklyn's Rose Water, came across it in the Campanile kitchen where he used to work. It's becoming popular on the East Coast, too, thanks to vegivores like Macris and farmers such as Rick Bishop of Mountain Sweet Berry Farm in Roscoe, New York, who recently added the aristocratic green to his crops. Its flavor is sweet and delicate and less bitter than most broccoli rabe, or, as Bishop says, "kalelike but better."

Bret Macris's Sautéed Spigarello with Chile Flakes and Honey

2 bunches Spigarello

1 tablespoon extra-virgin olive oil

1 teaspoon minced shallot

1 teaspoon minced garlic

Pinch of chile flakes

Salt and freshly ground black pepper to taste

Lemon juice to taste

1 tablespoon honey

Coarse sea salt to finish

Cut off the lower stems of the Spigarello leaves. (If the leaves are large and the stems tough throughout, remove them completely, as you might from kale.) Blanch the leaves and drain them in a colander, or dry them on paper towels or in a salad spinner. Heat olive oil in a large sauté pan over medium-high heat. Just before the oil starts to smoke, add the Spigarello and cook until slightly brown around the edges and a little crisp. Add the shallot, garlic, and chile flakes. Lower heat to medium or medium-low and cook, but don't brown the shallot and garlic. Season with salt and pepper and a squeeze of lemon juice. Plate the Spigarello, drizzle with honey, and sprinkle a little sea salt over the top. *Serves 4.*

CARROTS

A victim of its own nutritional profile, the carrot is too often relegated to its raw, rabbit-food status. But when chefs regard the root as something other than a beta-carotene delivery system, great things ensue. For one: this vibrantly seasoned salad from Israeli chef Einat Admony, who features it at her bustling New York falafel joint, Taïm. And if you thought sautéing carrots in oil negated their benefits, think again; the process actually renders their nutrients more accessible.

Einat Admony's Spicy Moroccan Carrots

2 pounds carrots

3 tablespoons olive oil, plus more for
    sautéing

½ tablespoon cumin

½ tablespoon paprika

½ tablespoon salt

½ teaspoon sugar

½ teaspoon freshly ground black pepper

3 garlic cloves, thinly sliced

Pinch of cayenne pepper

3 tablespoons white wine (or
    Champagne) vinegar

Peel carrots and place them in a large pot of cold water. Bring to a boil and cook carrots until slightly tender but not overdone, approximately 15 minutes depending on their size. Drain and place carrots in an ice-water bath until cool, then slice diagonally into ¼-inch-thick rounds. In a large pan, sauté the carrot slices in olive oil until slightly brown, cooking them in small batches if your pan becomes crowded. Place carrots in a bowl, add the olive oil and the remaining ingredients, and mix well. For best results, refrigerate, covered, overnight and serve at room temperature. *Serves 5.*

CAULIFLOWER

Although it's a year-round supermarket staple, cauliflower seems to evoke autumn, roasting, and creamy sauces. Which isn't to say you couldn't approach the vegetable in an entirely different way, as Boulud Sud chef Aaron Chambers does in this riff on a Middle Eastern–inspired tabbouleh salad. By pulsing the crucifer in a food processor, he manages the neat trick of making it resemble the dish's traditional bulgur wheat, which it crunchily replaces. Fresh herbs, dried fruit, and a citrusy dressing complete the illusion.

Aaron Chambers's Cauliflower Tabbouleh

2 heads of cauliflower

5 tablespoons extra-virgin olive oil

2 garlic cloves, minced

½ cup minced onion

Salt and freshly ground white pepper

¼ cup dried barberries (or chopped golden raisins)

5 dried figs, finely chopped

5 dried apricots, finely chopped

1 lemon, juice and zest

1½ tablespoons *za'atar* spice

3 tablespoons chopped parsley leaves

2 tablespoons chopped mint leaves

3 tablespoons chopped cilantro leaves

Trim the florets from the cauliflower and discard stalks and stems. Place florets in a food processor, and pulse until finely minced and approximately the size of couscous. Heat 2 tablespoons of olive oil in a sauté pan over medium heat; add garlic and onion, and sauté until translucent. Add the cauliflower, season with salt and pepper, and sauté for 2 to 3 minutes, stirring occasionally. The cauliflower should be just barely cooked. Transfer the cauliflower to a large bowl, and add barberries, figs, and apricots. In a small bowl, whisk together lemon juice, zest, remaining olive oil, and *za'atar* spice. No more than 1 hour before serving, add the lemon dressing, parsley, mint, and cilantro to the cauliflower and stir until combined. Season to taste with salt and pepper. *Serves 6.*

CHESTNUTS

Chestnut season need not begin and end with the Thanksgiving stuffing. Even if you don't have an open fire at your disposal, chestnuts roasting on a baking sheet in a 400-degree oven for twenty minutes and gobbled straight from their shells make for a pretty terrific holiday snack. But why stop there? Del Posto pastry chef Brooks Headley recommends steaming the starchy nuggets until they are meltingly soft, then hand-crushing them and seasoning them with citrus zest. The result, spooned over a little sweetened mascarpone, "is like a gremolata, a potato salad, and a dessert all in one," he says.

Brooks Headley's Spezzata di Castagne
with Zested Mascarpone

FOR THE STEAMED CHESTNUTS

1 pound fresh chestnuts, steamed or boiled in their shells

Salt and freshly ground black pepper to taste

1 to 1½ tablespoons extra-virgin olive oil

Zest of 2 tangerines

2 shakes of white wine vinegar

FOR THE ZESTED MASCARPONE

1 pound good mascarpone cheese

2 tablespoons turbinado sugar, plus more for garnish

Zest of 3 Meyer lemons

Zest of 3 tangerines

Pinch of salt

FOR THE CHESTNUTS: Cut the chestnuts in half while still warm and remove the meat. Tear the chestnuts into large pieces and season with salt and pepper to taste. Dress lightly with olive oil, the tangerine zest, and the vinegar. Toss to combine.

FOR THE ZESTED MASCARPONE: Combine all the ingredients and fluff together with a fork, without dissolving the sugar.

TO SERVE: Spoon 2 tablespoons of the zested mascarpone on a plate. Save the remaning mascarpone mixture for another use. Top with a mound of the seasoned chestnuts. Sprinkle a few more grains of sugar over the top. Serve immediately. *Serves 4 to 6.*

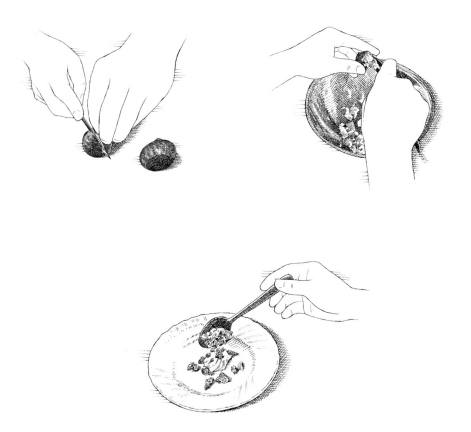

CARDOONS

Revered in France, Spain, and especially Italy for its slightly bitter and herby flavor, the cardoon has only recently begun to make a name for itself on American menus. The fact that this close relative of the globe artichoke looks like a giant head of celery that's been run through the wringer can't have helped. But chances are wherever there are hungry enclaves of Italian expats and first-generation Italian-Americans, you'll find locally grown specimens of the exotic thistle. Make its acquaintance in traditional, typically cold-weather preparations, like the warm garlic-and-oil vegetable dip called *bagna cauda*, or cloaked under a creamy *fonduta* in this classic Piedmontese recipe from Al di Là's Anna Klinger.

Anna Klinger's Cardoons with Fonduta

1 large bunch cardoons

Juice of half a lemon

1 tablespoon, plus a pinch salt

4 cups milk

8 tablespoons (1 stick) butter (or truffle
  butter, optional)

4 ounces (¾ cup) flour

6 ounces Fontina cheese,
  grated

½ cup Parmesan cheese,
  grated

Slice the cardoons across the base and trim the tips, removing leaves and any brown edges. Discard any hollow stalks, retaining only the firm pale-green ones. With a vegetable peeler, peel the stalks, removing the tough strings. Cut crosswise into 2-inch pieces, and place in a bowl of cold water along with the lemon juice. Leave to soak overnight or for at least 6 hours in the refrigerator. Drain and place in a large pot with fresh cold water with a pinch of salt. Bring to a boil and simmer until tender (depending on the cardoons, this might take anywhere from a half hour to an hour), then drain. While the cardoons are cooking, preheat the oven to 375 degrees and make the sauce: In a saucepot, add the salt to the milk and gently heat. In a 4-quart saucepot, melt the butter over low heat. Slowly sprinkle flour into the melted butter, stirring constantly with a wooden spoon to avoid lumps. When the mixture is smooth and shiny, begin to add the warm milk a little at a time, again stirring constantly. Continue to heat and stir until mixture is almost at a boil. Add the grated Fontina and allow it to melt into the sauce. Place the cardoons in a bowl and strain the sauce into the bowl, mixing well with the cardoons. Arrange cardoons in a buttered gratin dish. Sprinkle with grated Parmesan and bake until golden brown, about a half hour. *Serves 4.*

PURPLE CARROTS

Before carrots were orange, they were purple—not unlike the ones you'll find at the Paffen-roth Gardens farmstand at New York City's Greenmarket. With a striking shade of mauve on the outside and a deep-orange interior, they're sweeter, crisper, and more nutritious than the average carrot. Standard Grill chef Dan Silverman is a fan. And so are the Orange County deer that prowl the Paffenroth property like bandits. According to owner Alex Paffenroth, these culi-narily advanced ruminants focus their attentions exclusively on the purples, ignoring entirely the white, yellow, and orange varieties.

Dan Silverman's Purple-Carrot and Purslane Salad

1 bunch purslane

2 purple carrots

3 to 4 ounces feta cheese, diced into
  half-inch pieces, for serving

2 tablespoons pine nuts, toasted, for
  serving

Salt and pepper

FOR THE VINAIGRETTE

3½ tablespoons extra-virgin olive oil

1 tablespoon red-wine vinegar

1 tablespoon chopped fresh oregano leaves

1 tablespoon minced shallot

Remove big stems from the purslane and wash in a salad spinner. Wash carrots well and trim tops. Slice carrots very thin lengthwise with a mandoline, shock in an ice-water bath, spin dry, and combine with purslane in a large bowl. Season with salt and pepper. In a small bowl, whisk in the olive oil with the vinegar, oregano, shallot, and salt and pepper. Toss with the purslane and carrots. To serve: Plate salad and sprinkle with feta and pine nuts. ***Serves 2.***

CRABAPPLES

Small in size, mealy in texture, and high in pectin, crabapples are bad for eating out of hand but great for jam. Patti Jackson, the ambidextrous pastry and savory chef and veteran of such Manhattan kitchens as Mad.61, Alto, Centovini, and i Trulli, cooks them into *mostarda*, a chutneylike Italian condiment that pairs well with sheep's-milk cheese or *bollito misto*. Horseradish, ginger, red pepper, and mustard oil lend a savory bite and distinctive flavor profile, making the spicy stuff a great holiday gift.

Patti Jackson's Crabapple Mostarda

5 pounds firm crabapples

Juice of 1 lemon

3 cups sugar

2 bay leaves

2 cinnamon sticks

1 (2-inch) piece horseradish root, quartered

1 (1-inch) piece fresh ginger, quartered

1 teaspoon dried red pepper flakes

1 tablespoon mustard oil or wasabi oil

Wash 3 pounds of crabapples, and remove stem and blossom ends (do not pare or core); reserve remaining fruit. Cut the trimmed apples into quarters and place in a pot. Add two quarts of water, cover, and bring to a boil, stirring frequently. Reduce heat and simmer for 20 to 25 minutes, or until crabapples are just soft; do not overcook. When fruit is tender, pour contents of pot through a triple layer of dampened cheesecloth into a large container. Tie the cheesecloth to a wooden spoon and position over container to drain without pressing or squeezing, yielding 4 cups of juice. (Discard cheesecloth contents, or use for applesauce.) Wash, peel, and dice the remaining crabapples and toss with lemon juice. Bring the drained juice and sugar to a boil over medium-high heat. Add the bay leaves, cinnamon sticks, horseradish, ginger, and pepper flakes. When the juice reaches 218 degrees or drips thickly off a metal spoon, remove the horseradish, cinnamon, ginger, and bay leaves. Add the diced fruit. Stir, and continue cooking for 8 to 9 minutes. Add the mustard oil or wasabi oil. Pour into canning jars, following manufacturer's instructions, or store in a glass or plastic container in the refrigerator. ***Makes approximately 6 cups.***

FENNEL

Crunchy-bulbed and frilly-fronded, fennel is a tad misunderstood. A member of the parsley family with a subtle licorice flavor, it's often misidentified as anise, another plant entirely. Most Americans know it for its seed, a major player in Italian sausage. But it's just as memorable braised, or in crisp salads like the one Caroline Fidanza constructed as opening chef at Williamsburg's Diner, fashioned from ultrathin slices of fennel and celery heaped on a bed of silky prosciutto.

Caroline Fidanza's Fennel Salad

1 large fennel bulb, fronds reserved

2 celery ribs, leaves reserved

1 teaspoon kosher salt

¼ cup fresh lemon juice

3 tablespoons extra-virgin olive oil

8 slices prosciutto

Freshly ground black pepper

Halve, core, and thinly slice fennel bulb (preferably with a mandoline). Slice celery diagonally into long, thin slices. Salt vegetables and toss with lemon juice and olive oil. To serve, arrange prosciutto slices on a platter, mound vegetables on top, season with pepper, and garnish with celery leaves and fennel fronds. *Serves 4.*

FRESH GINGER

*I*n what might qualify as the most surprising crop to materialize at a New York City Greenmarket, ginger has begun to be harvested by a couple of local farms run by Korean immigrants, both specializing in Asian varieties of produce. Should you live in an area likewise unexpectedly blessed with the presence of the gnarled rhizome, which tends to be grown in tropical and subtropical climes, try infusing it into this hot herbal tea, the perfect elixir for a rainy fall day.

Balthazar Bakery's Ginger Citrus Tea

4 cups water

⅛ cinnamon stick

5 ounces fresh ginger

¼ lemon, peel only, zested in strips

¼ cup freshly squeezed lemon juice
  (about 1½ lemons)

⅓ cup honey

¼ bunch fresh mint, washed

Bring water to a boil with cinnamon. Peel ginger with a spoon, paring knife, or vegetable peeler. Roughly chop the ginger and add to the pot along with lemon zest and juice. Cover and simmer for 30 minutes. Add honey, stir well, and simmer, covered, for another 20 minutes. Pour over fresh mint, then strain and serve, or allow to cool and refrigerate. ***Makes about 1 quart.***

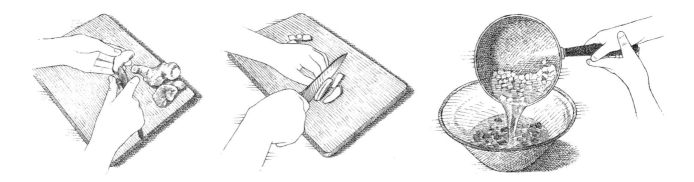

CRANBERRIES

Like roast turkey and sweet potatoes, cranberries are often relegated to holiday status. That's a shame, since the native North American berries have a tart brightness that can wake up meat or grain dishes, or add a lively spark to any number of desserts. For a quick fix, we recommend this winterized caipirinha, made with fresh cranberries, by the folks at Ideya Latin Bistro, a Soho, New York, spot known for its tropical libations. Look for native heirloom varieties at your local farmers' market (if you live in the vicinity of bogs in Massachusetts, Wisconsin, or the Pacific Northwest), and muddle them with citrus and sugar for deliciously sweet-tart proof that you needn't limit your cranberry consumption to one day a year.

Ideya's Cranberry Caipirinha

1 or 2 lime wedges (to taste)

1 small orange wedge

10 cranberries

1 tablespoon brown sugar

1 ounce fresh lime juice

1.5 ounces aged cachaça

Place the lime, orange, and cranberries in a cocktail shaker. Add the sugar and muddle with the fruit. Fill a rocks glass with cracked ice and transfer the ice to the shaker. Add the lime juice and the cachaça and shake well. Pour everything, including all the muddled fruit from the shaker, into the rocks glass and serve. *Makes 1 drink.*

CROSNES

Sure, that pleasure-seeker who first slurped an oyster was an intrepid sort, but he had nothing on the fearless *fresser* who first tucked into a plate of crosnes (pronounced *crones*, and named after the town in France where the Asian export was first cultivated). Despite their wormy looks, the tiny tubers are prized by chefs for their nutty sunchoke-like flavor and crunchy radishy texture. Try them sautéed in butter, pickled, or in this unusual, tropics-inspired dessert soup from Annisa's Anita Lo.

Anita Lo's Chilled Coconut-Fruit Soup with Mint and Crosnes

1 (14-ounce) can unsweetened coconut milk

2½ cups milk

½ cup sugar, or to taste

Pinch of salt

½ cup crosnes, cleaned and, if large, cut into bite-size pieces

2 cups fruit like pineapple, mango, or even avocado, diced

4 large mint leaves, chopped

Place coconut milk, milk, sugar, and salt in a pot and bring to a boil. Remove to a bowl and chill. In a small pot, place crosnes in cold water and bring to a boil, then drain. Mix the fruit and the crosnes with the coconut-milk mixture. Divide among 4 bowls and garnish with mint. ***Serves 4.***

HEN-OF-THE-WOODS MUSHROOMS

The Japanese *maitake* mushroom earned its alias, hen-of-the-woods, from a supposed resemblance to a hen's body. Flavorwise, it's rich and earthy, traits only enhanced in the hands of Marco Canora, the chef largely responsible for elevating the variety to its lofty status among New York fungus fiends, first at Craft and now at Hearth. Serve his pan-roasted *maitake* as a side, but take note: the deep, funky, faintly crisp-on-the-outside-juicy-within results might very well upstage the main event.

Marco Canora's Pan-Roasted Hen-of-the-Woods Mushrooms

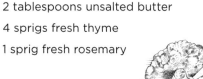

1 pound hen-of-the-woods mushrooms

¼ cup extra-virgin olive oil

2 tablespoons kosher salt

2 tablespoons fresh-cracked black pepper

2 tablespoons unsalted butter

4 sprigs fresh thyme

1 sprig fresh rosemary

Turn mushroom over to expose the stem. With paring knife, remove the core of the stem. Using your hands, gently break mushroom into 8 pieces. In a 12-inch sauté pan, heat olive oil over medium flame. Season mushrooms with salt and pepper and place them in the heated oil, taking care not to overcrowd the pan, and cook for 3 minutes. When the mushrooms have a golden-brown surface, flip them with a spatula and continue cooking for 2 to 3 minutes. Add butter and herbs, and baste mushrooms for 1 minute. Drain on paper towels to remove excess oil, discard thyme and rosemary sprigs, and serve. *Serves 4.*

HONEYCRISP APPLES

Developed by University of Minnesota breeders in 1960 and introduced in 1991, the Honeycrisp apple is an extraordinarily crunchy cross between the Macoun and the Honeygold. Its crisp, juicy texture makes it a superb eating apple, but when Monkey Bar chef Damon Wise was cooking at Tom Colicchio's Craft, he liked to amp up the fruit's sweet, slightly tart flavor in a savory cake of herb-dappled slices slow-baked in duck fat.

Damon Wise's Apple Confit Cake

5 medium Honeycrisp apples

¼ pound duck fat or butter

Salt and freshly ground black pepper

⅛ cup fresh thyme leaves

⅛ cup chopped chives

Preheat oven to 275 degrees. Peel and core apples. Melt duck fat or butter in small saucepan over low heat. Coat a 6-inch straight-sided pie tin with a bit of the duck fat or butter using a paper towel. Working quickly so that apples don't oxidize, slice them into thin rings using a mandoline. Make a layer of apple rings in the bottom of the pie tin, overlapping so that no holes are visible, then season with salt and pepper, sprinkle with about a quarter of the herbs, and drizzle with 1 teaspoon of duck fat or butter. Continue to layer, season, sprinkle, and drizzle until you've used all the apple rings. Press top layer with hands so that the surface is even. Cover with parchment paper that has been cut to fit inside the pie tin. Cut a penny-size hole in the center of the parchment to let steam escape. Bake for 2½ hours, until soft. Remove from oven and let stand for 30 minutes. Gently flip onto a plate, and serve sliced with roasted foie gras, sweetbreads, venison, or duck breast. (The cake may also be refrigerated and served cold.) ***Serves 6 to 8.***

JAPANESE SWEET POTATOES

If spring is all about asparagus and summer is a toss-up between corn and tomatoes, then fall rightly belongs to sweet potatoes—but not just the familiar orange-fleshed variety so obligatory at Thanksgiving. The type known variously as *satsuma-imo*, or Japanese sweet potato, has a dense, starchy flesh and superb chestnutlike flavor. It's delicious baked in its skin or cooked in cream the way Hearth chef Marco Canora does.

Marco Canora's Japanese Sweet Potato Gratin

4 pounds Japanese
   sweet potatoes, peeled
2 quarts heavy cream
5 ounces prosciutto, cut in
   large dice

½ bunch sage, tied with string
Salt and freshly ground white
   pepper to taste

Preheat oven to 350 degrees. Using a mandoline, slice sweet potatoes about ⅛ inch thick. Place sweet potato slices in a heavy-bottomed pot and cover with cream. Add prosciutto and sage and season to taste. Simmer over medium heat until tender, about 20 minutes. With a slotted spoon, remove prosciutto and sage and discard. Remove sweet potatoes from pot, reserving 1 cup of the cream. Layer the potato slices evenly in an 9-by-13-inch baking dish. Pour the reserved cup of cream over the potatoes and let it settle for 5 minutes. Place baking dish in oven for 15 minutes, until potatoes are golden brown. ***Serves 6 to 8.***

KABOCHA SQUASH

Of all the edible gourds on riotous display at the fall farmers' market, kabocha squash is one of the sweetest. Motorino and Bowery Diner chef-owner Mathieu Palombino plays up that flavor by roasting the dry-textured flesh, then garnishing it with a sticky balsamic reduction and shavings of salty cheese. Once you manage to peel off the plant's tough skin with a sharp, sturdy knife, the recipe couldn't be simpler.

Mathieu Palombino's
Roasted Kabocha Squash

1 kabocha squash (2½ to 3 pounds)

1 garlic clove, chopped

½ cup extra-virgin olive oil

Salt and freshly ground black pepper

2 cups balsamic vinegar, reduced to ½ cup

2 ounces Parmigiano-Reggiano cheese

½ bunch fresh oregano

Preheat oven to 400 degrees. Split the squash lengthwise; remove seeds and skin. Slice the squash into ½-inch-thick pieces. Place them in a large bowl. Add the garlic and half the olive oil, and season with salt and pepper. Toss until well coated. Arrange squash on a baking sheet so that the pieces aren't touching, and roast them for about 20 to 30 minutes or until lightly browned on top and well browned on bottom. Let cool for about 15 minutes, then arrange on a plate. Drizzle with balsamic reduction, and shave the Parmigiano-Reggiano on top. Garnish with a few oregano leaves and drizzle with the remaining olive oil. *Serves 4 to 6 as an appetizer or side.*

JERUSALEM ARTICHOKES

Neither from Jerusalem nor an artichoke, this native American tuber is actually a kind of sunflower, or *girasole* in Italian. The sunchoke, as it's also known, is nutty, rich in iron, and satisfyingly crunchy, a trait Betto chef Shaunna Sargent exploits to delicious effect in this refreshing autumn salad, where the sunchoke is paired with pears and hazelnuts, and garnished with a garlicky sunchoke purée.

Shaunna Sargent's Sunchokes and Pears

FOR PURÉE

4 medium sunchokes (or enough to
    yield 2 cups cut into ¼-inch slices)
2 shallots, thinly sliced
2 garlic cloves, smashed

2 sprigs thyme
Salt and freshly ground pepper
⅓ cup plus 2 tablespoons olive oil
1 cup whole milk

FOR SALAD

2 large sunchokes, scrubbed well
2 large, ripe Bosc pears
½ cup hazelnuts, toasted and roughly
    chopped
2 tablespoons grated pecorino cheese
Juice of half a lemon

2 tablespoons white wine vinegar
2 tablespoons olive oil, plus more
    to finish
1 tablespoon chopped tarragon
Salt and freshly ground black pepper

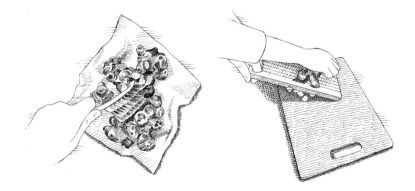
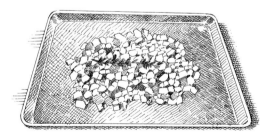

FOR PURÉE: Preheat oven to 350 degrees. Scrub the sunchokes well, and cut into ¼-inch slices. In a medium-size bowl, toss together sunchokes, shallots, garlic, thyme, salt and pepper, and 2 tablespoons olive oil. Lay out on a baking sheet and roast until sunchokes are slightly golden brown and tender to touch, about 15 to 20 minutes. Remove thyme. Place everything in a small pot and cover with milk, bring to a simmer, and cook an additional 20 minutes. Transfer to a blender and blend until very smooth. Finish with ⅓ cup olive oil. Let cool.

FOR SALAD: Slice sunchokes and pears on a mandoline to about the thickness of a quarter. Add the hazelnuts, pecorino, lemon juice, vinegar, 2 tablespoons olive oil, tarragon, and salt and pepper and toss together.

TO PLATE: Spoon about ¼ cup of purée onto each plate, arrange salad delicately on top and around, and drizzle with a little more purée. Finish with more pepper and olive oil. ***Serves 4.***

KOHLRABI

*I*t's tough being a stem. You go through life supporting a family of leaves, buds, shoots, what have you, only to be separated from them in the end and unceremoniously tossed into the trash. Not so the radishlike kohlrabi, whose best part is a bulb that is, technically speaking, 100 percent stem. The tennis-ball–size brassica (its name is German for "cabbage turnip") is crisp, juicy, and delicately sweet—all qualities that make it a nifty substitute for cucumber in this *tzatziki* recipe from Charles Brassard of Brooklyn's Café Colette.

Charles Brassard's Kohlrabi Tzatziki

4 medium kohlrabi

3 garlic cloves, finely chopped

1 tablespoon salt, plus more to taste

1 quart Greek yogurt

¼ cup lemon juice

¼ cup roughly chopped mint

Extra-virgin olive oil, to taste

Freshly ground black pepper to taste

Cut the leaves off the kohlrabi and save them for another use. Peel away the tough outer skin. Cut bulbs into large pieces and coarsely grate them. In a bowl, combine grated kohlrabi, chopped garlic, and 1 tablespoon of salt and let sit for 15 minutes to draw out liquid. Strain or squeeze out liquid and discard. Toss kohlrabi with yogurt, lemon juice, mint, and a drizzle of olive oil. Season with salt and pepper. Serve as a side with grilled fish or meats, especially lamb. ***Serves 6.***

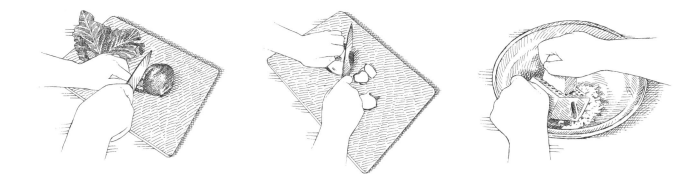

LAKEMONT
GRAPES

Nothing signals the beginning of autumn in New York farmers' markets like the return of native American grapes (primarily *Vitis labrusca*). Del Posto pastry chef Brooks Headley likes to freeze a seedless variety, like Jupiter or Lakemont (or Canadice, Mars, Himrod—take your pick), until the grapes transform into what he calls "frosty sorbet bombs" encased in skins with "an almost Gray's Papaya–like snap." The whipped-cream-cheese garnish is flavored with wild fennel pollen for an Italian-cheesecake effect.

Brooks Headley's Frozen Lakemont Grapes with Whipped Fennel-Pollen Cream Cheese

2 bunches Lakemont grapes

8 ounces cream cheese

¼ cup sugar

Pinch of kosher salt

4 ounces crème fraîche

½ teaspoon wild fennel pollen

Arrange grapes in a single layer on a baking sheet and freeze for 3 hours. Soften cream cheese in a mixing bowl with a rubber spatula. Add remaining ingredients and whisk until fluffy. Chill for 30 minutes. Top with frozen grapes; serve immediately. ***Serves 6 to 8.***

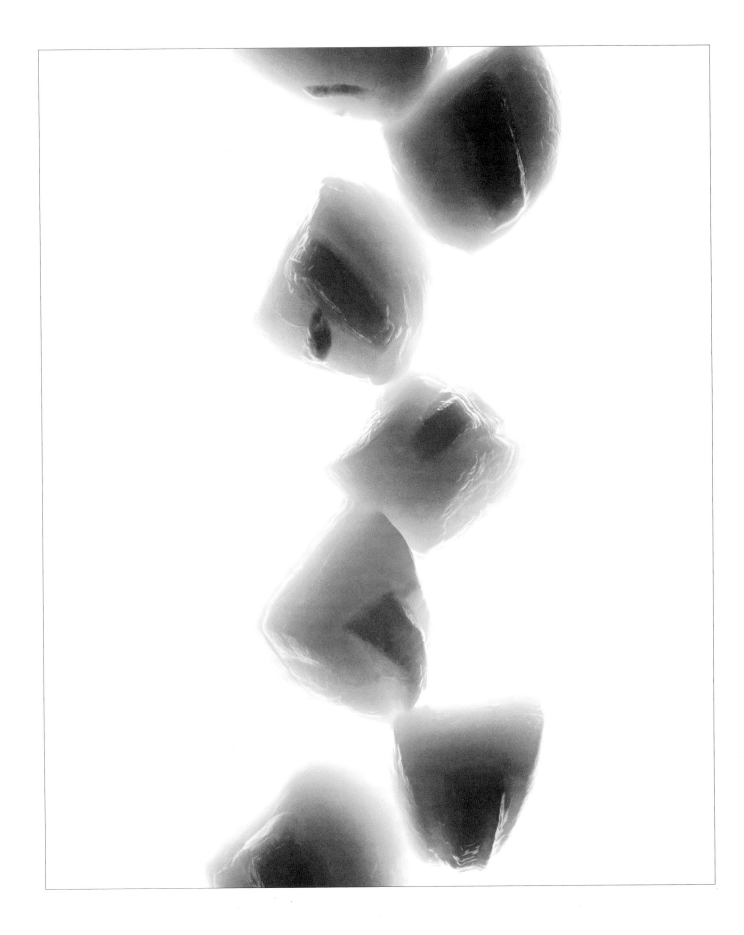

NANTUCKET BAY SCALLOPS

Smaller and sweeter than their seafaring cousins, Nantucket Bay scallops are prized for their tender texture and refined flavor, which means they require little culinary intervention. Butter, oil, salt and pepper, a hot pan, and the following recipe from Oceana chef Ben Pollinger are all you really need to do the succulent mini-mollusks justice.

Ben Pollinger's Nantucket Bay Scallops with Caramelized Figs

8 Kadota or Black Mission figs

2 tablespoons sugar

5 tablespoons vegetable oil

1 cup arugula

2 teaspoons extra-virgin olive oil

1 pound Nantucket Bay scallops

Salt and freshly ground black pepper
   to taste

4 tablespoons butter

Wash figs, remove stems, and halve lengthwise. Dip cut sides lightly in sugar and set aside. Heat a heavy 10-inch skillet over medium heat and add 1 tablespoon of vegetable oil, so the surface is lightly coated. Add figs, cut side down, and cook until lightly caramelized. Flip figs and cook for an additional 30 seconds, remove from pan, and reserve. Toss arugula with olive oil and reserve. Season scallops lightly with salt and pepper. Wipe sugar residue from skillet and place over medium-high heat, adding remaining 4 tablespoons vegetable oil plus butter and swirling the skillet until the butter melts and begins to brown. Add scallops and cook for 1 to 3 minutes (until opaque), constantly swirling the pan so that the scallops are rolling around. Remove scallops to a paper-towel-lined plate. Divide arugula among 4 plates, then scatter scallops and figs among the greens. *Serves 4.*

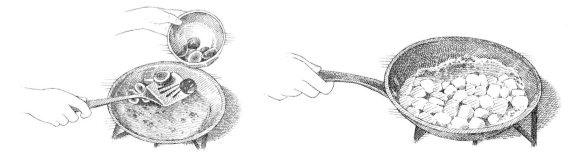

ORANGE CAULIFLOWER

*I*f cauliflower is nothing but cabbage with a college education, as Mark Twain once said, then is orange cauliflower just cabbage that went down to Fort Lauderdale for spring break and came back with a funny tan? Well, maybe, but cheery good looks aside, this George Hamilton of the Cruciferae family has about twenty-five times more vitamin A than the plain old white variety. Some say it also has a sweeter flavor—one that Barbuto's Jonathan Waxman plays up by pan-roasting, and complements with a garlicky anchovy sauce.

Jonathan Waxman's Pan-Roasted Cauliflower with Anchovy

2 small heads of orange cauliflower (white or purple will do in a pinch)

2 garlic cloves, peeled, cored, and
   crushed

6 anchovy fillets

½ cup extra-virgin olive oil

Half a lemon

Salt and freshly ground black pepper to taste

Preheat oven to 425 degrees. Wash and dry the cauliflower and cut the leaves away. Detach the stem by making a cone-shaped incision into the bottom of the cauliflower, and pull away the large florets, then cut them into bite-size pieces. Using a mortar and pestle, mash garlic and anchovies with ¼ cup of the olive oil, adding lemon juice to taste. In a large, heavy, ovenproof skillet, heat the remaining ¼ cup olive oil. Add cauliflower, season with salt and pepper, and sauté for 2 minutes, then pan-roast in oven until golden brown for approximately 10 minutes. Add ¼ cup cold water, lower heat to 350, and continue cooking for 30 minutes, turning florets occasionally, until brown and tender. Remove from oven, place on a large platter, and drizzle with the anchovy sauce. *Serves 4.*

PURPLE MAJESTY POTATOES

Not only does the Purple Majesty come in a shade of violet so striking that even Prince would say it is a bit much, it's also really good for you. The potato was developed in 2006 by Colorado growers using natural cross-breeding techniques that somehow resulted in a superspud containing freakishly high amounts of antioxidants.

They're great fried, but Gramercy Tavern's Michael Anthony recommends a simple method inspired by a guest-chef visit from the late, great Bernard Loiseau. The backstory: At first, Anthony couldn't believe that Loiseau had traveled all the way from France to crush potatoes with a fork. But when he saw the intensity with which the Frenchman approached his task, and how much attention he lavished on such a humble ingredient, it won him over. A smashing tip: never overwork the potatoes; use a crushing, not a mixing, motion.

Michael Anthony's Fork-Crushed Purple Majesty Potatoes

1 pound Purple Majesty potatoes,
   washed
Kosher salt
4 small shallots, minced
2 tablespoons fresh lemon juice

6 tablespoons extra-virgin olive oil
Fleur de sel to taste
Freshly ground white pepper
   to taste
2 tablespoons chopped parsley

In a large pot, cook potatoes with skins on in heavily salted boiling water until tender, approximately 15 minutes. Remove potatoes from pot, and peel them while still warm. Place potatoes in a large bowl and, using a fork, gently smash them, maintaining a fairly chunky consistency. Fold in minced shallots, lemon juice, olive oil, fleur de sel, and white pepper. Finish with parsley. *Serves 4.*

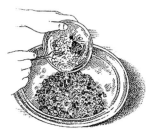

POMEGRANATES

*F*or many, there are few kitchen chores as dreaded as extracting the juicy, jewel-like seeds from a pomegranate. A tip: Do not perform this dirty deed while wearing your favorite white shirt. Another: Submerge the fruit in a bowl of water, as demonstrated below, and you'll lessen the likelihood of making a horrible mess. Once you pry the seeds away from their pithy pods, try them in this autumnal salad adapted from Dieci, one of New York's few Italian-Japanese restaurants.

Dieci's Smoked-Duck Salad with Persimmons and Pomegranates

Juice of 2 oranges

1 tablespoon veal stock (optional)

1 tablespoon coarse-grained mustard

¾ cup extra-virgin olive oil

Salt and freshly ground black pepper
    to taste

1 pomegranate (for ½ cup pomegranate
    seeds; you can freeze the remaining
    seeds for up to 6 months)

2 small ripe Fuyu persimmons

1 smoked duck breast (available from
    dartagnan.com)

2 bunches arugula, washed and dried

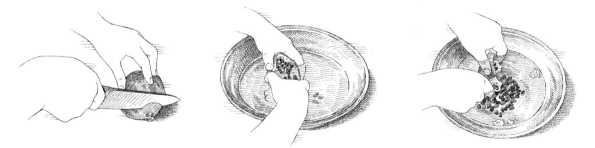

FOR THE DRESSING: In a small pot, simmer orange juice over medium heat for 5 to 7 minutes, until reduced by approximately half. Let juice cool in a bowl. Add veal stock, mustard, olive oil, and salt and pepper and whisk together well.

TO EXTRACT THE POMEGRANATE SEEDS: Slice off the crown end of the fruit and score the rind in quarters. In a large bowl filled with water, gently break the fruit apart into 4 pieces. Bend the skin side of the segments inside out, separating the seeds from the membranes. Skim off the pith, which will float to the top. Drain the seeds into a colander.

Peel and slice persimmons lengthwise. Thinly slice the duck breast. Place persimmon, pomegranate seeds, arugula, and duck slices in a large bowl, and toss with the dressing. Adjust seasoning. *Serves 4.*

QUINCE

Although the ancient Romans went for them in a big way, most folks today don't know what to make of this superbly scented—but in its raw form, basically inedible—fruit. An inspired suggestion from British food writer Kate Whiteman: shove one in your glove compartment to deodorize your car. (Now *there's* an idea for the New York City Taxi & Limousine Commission.) An even better one comes from Andrew Carmellini circa his Café Boulud days: gently poach with honey and spices and serve as a sweet-tart accompaniment to wild game, pot roast, or pork chops, or simply spread on toast.

Andrew Carmellini's Quince in Wine and Roses

5 quinces, peeled, quartered, and cored, peels reserved

Freshly squeezed juice of 5 lemons

1 cup red, white, or sweet wine

1 cup honey

3 whole star anise, crushed

1 cinnamon stick, crushed

½ teaspoon rosewater

Cut each quince into 12 wedges and place in a large nonreactive bowl. Add the juice of 1 lemon and enough water to cover. In a large pot, combine 2 quarts water with remaining lemon juice, quince peels, wine, honey, star anise, and cinnamon. Bring to a boil and reduce liquid by half, then strain through mesh sieve, discarding star anise and cinnamon. Return liquid to pot. Drain quinces, add to pot, and bring to a boil. Cook quince over medium heat until tender, about 10 minutes. With a slotted spoon, transfer quince to a large nonreactive container. Bring liquid to a boil and reduce until it reaches a syruplike consistency. Stir in rosewater and pour the syrup over the quince. Let cool to room temperature, cover, and refrigerate. *Serves 4.*

SECKEL PEARS

Fall is the perfect time to expand your pear horizons, when farmers' market stands are overflowing not only with Boscs and Bartletts, but also Clapps, Devoes, and Seckels—those chubby little "sugar pears" known for their grainy texture and spicy-sweet flavor. City Bakery alum Ilene Rosen, now the chef/co-owner of 606 R&D in Brooklyn, likes to slice them in half and bake them—stem, seeds, and all—with maple syrup and butter for a simple fall dessert that's even better paired with creamy Camembert from Old Chatham Sheepherding Company.

Ilene Rosen's
Maple Butter–Baked Seckel Pears

6 to 10 medium to larger-size Seckel pears, stems on

4 tablespoons unsalted butter

3 tablespoons maple syrup (preferably grade B or dark amber)

Salt and freshly ground black pepper

Preheat oven to 400 degrees. Cut pears in half lengthwise. Brown butter in a small saucepan, and combine in a bowl with the maple syrup. Mix well. Toss pears in bowl to coat with mixture, and sprinkle with salt and pepper. Place pears on a baking sheet, cut side down, and bake 20 minutes, until pears are soft and cut side is very soft and caramelized. Let cool briefly before serving. **Serves 4 to 6.**

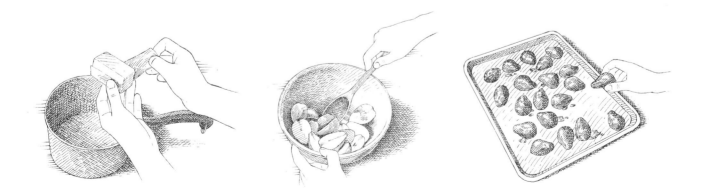

SUGAR PUMPKINS

Smaller, sweeter, and much more flavorful than the standard supersize variety, sugar pumpkins are also less stringy and have a higher flesh-to-seed-cavity ratio. They're good for pie-making or any recipe that calls for an exceptionally smooth purée, like the pumpkin pastry cream that Food Network personality Amanda Freitag features in her individual-size versions of *zuccotto*, the dome-shaped molded Florentine dessert.

Amanda Freitag's Pumpkin Zuccotto

1 3- to-4-pound sugar pumpkin

1 cup milk

2 tablespoons plus 1 teaspoon
   cornstarch

⅓ cup sugar

½ teaspoon vanilla extract

1 egg

2 egg yolks

2 tablespoons unsalted butter

¼ teaspoon ground cinnamon

1 teaspoon honey

Pinch of nutmeg

Pinch of salt

¼ cup Nutella

16 ladyfingers

2 cups Marsala

Cocoa powder, for serving

Confectioners' sugar, for serving

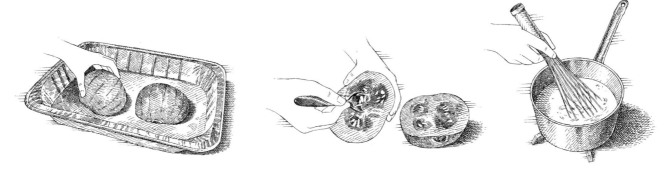

Preheat oven to 350 degrees.

TO MAKE THE PUMPKIN-PURÉE BASE: Cut the pumpkin in half and remove seeds. Place the pumpkin in a in roasting pan, flesh side down, and cover with foil. Cook until tender, approximately 1 hour. When cool, scoop out flesh with a spoon and blend until smooth in a food processor.

TO MAKE THE PASTRY CREAM BASE: In a medium nonreactive saucepan, combine milk, cornstarch, sugar, and vanilla extract. Over medium heat, cook the mixture, whisking continuously, until it begins to thicken. Remove pan from heat and set aside. In a bowl, mix the egg and the egg yolks and whisk in ¼ cup of the warm milk mixture until thoroughly combined. Stir the egg mixture into the pan on low heat and cook until it becomes thick like custard. Remove from heat and stir in butter. (It should yield 1 cup.)

TO MAKE THE PUMPKIN PASTRY CREAM: Mix together the pumpkin purée, cinnamon, honey, nutmeg, and salt with ¾ cup of the pastry cream. Blend the remaining ¼ cup of pastry cream with the Nutella.

TO ASSEMBLE: Dip each ladyfinger in Marsala so it's moist but not soggy. Line each of 4 muffin molds by layering 3 ladyfingers on the bottom and sides of the mold to create a basket. Fill the lined mold half-way with pumpkin pastry cream, then place a dollop of the Nutella mixture in the center and finish with more pumpkin cream. Finally, break a fourth ladyfinger in half and layer over the top of each mold to close. Refrigerate the cakes for 1 hour. Remove from refrigerator and invert the muffin pan onto a sheet pan. Place the *zuccotto* cakes on plates and sprinkle with cocoa powder and confectioners' sugar. ***Serves 4.***

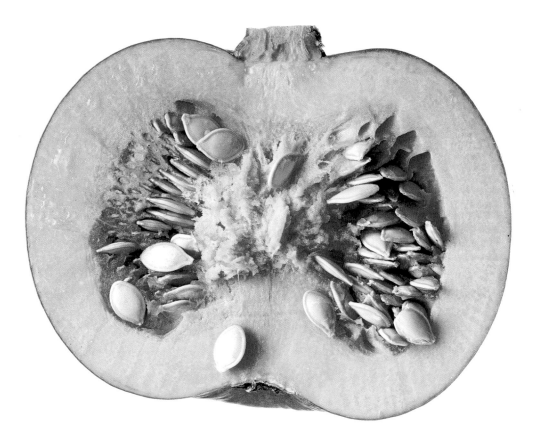

WALNUTS

While walnuts are available year-round, they're actually harvested in autumn, with the season's crop hitting shelves and the bowls of nutcracker-wielding fans just in time for the holidays. The nut, a powerhouse of omega-3 fatty acids and other good stuff, gets top billing in this vegan-soup recipe from Justin Hilbert, chef of Brooklyn's Gwynnett St.

Justin Hilbert's Walnut Soup

1 pound walnuts, chopped

1 medium white onion

5 celery stalks, leaves attached

¼ cup extra-virgin olive oil, plus 1½ tablespoons for sunchokes

1 cup cold water

3 Bartlett pears

1 quart soy milk, plus extra for consistency

Sea salt to taste

¼ pound sunchokes

4 pickled walnuts

Preheat oven to 400 degrees. In a medium pot, cover the walnut pieces with cold water and bring to a boil, then simmer for 5 minutes. Strain and spread walnuts over a baking sheet, toasting in oven to a golden brown, approximately 10 minutes. Dice the onion and the celery, reserving celery leaves for garnish. Add ¼ cup of olive oil to a soup pot and cook celery and onions over a low flame until soft, approximately 20 minutes. Add the toasted walnuts and the cold water, then boil for 3 minutes. Reduce heat and simmer until walnuts are soft, approximately 40 minutes. Remove from heat and let cool. Dice pears, reserving 1 for garnish, and blend the other 2 in a blender with the walnut mixture (blend in batches if necessary). Blend until smooth, slowly adding the soy milk. Season with sea salt. Strain contents of blender into a bowl, discarding pulp, and let chill over an ice bath. For garnish: Cut the sunchokes into bite-size rounds and toss with 1½ tablespoons of olive oil and a pinch of salt. Roast sunchokes at 400 degrees until golden brown and tender, about 10 minutes. Mince celery leaves and pickled walnuts and reserve. To serve: Warm soup, adding soy milk and salt if needed. Froth with a hand blender if desired, and garnish with warm roasted sunchokes, the remaining diced pear, pickled walnuts, and celery leaves. *Serves 4.*

*I*n the dead of winter I crave foods that are restorative. It might seem, at first, that there's little to work with: Many of the ingredients that are available at this time of year are kept in cellars from the time they were harvested at their peak in late summer or fall. These are fruits and vegetables with staying power—apples, squashes, root vegetables, and cabbage. Luckily, or perhaps by natural selection, these lend themselves well to restorative preparations such as warming soups or stews, long braises, or caramelizations. But what's a chef to do to create a balanced menu with lighter preparations? Thankfully, much can be grown at this time of year locally with the help of a covering such as a hoop house, a type of greenhouse made from a sheet of plastic reinforced by flexible piping. With this added protection, cold-weather greens such as kale, mustard greens, chicories, mâche and claytonia do well. And citrus is amazing at this time of year from down South or out West. I look forward to local seasonal fish such as pollock, Maine sweet shrimp, Peconic Bay scallops. Oysters are at their best, too. And black truffles from across the ocean. Is there anything better than oysters and black truffles with salsify? Or Peconic Bay scallops with braised escarole and *bottarga*? Or sweet shrimp raw with a little Meyer lemon? Or all the above shellfish with some pollock in a preserved kimchee stew? Food to make you feel alive—enough to sustain you until spring.

—ANITA LO, EXECUTIVE CHEF/OWNER, ANNISA

WINTER

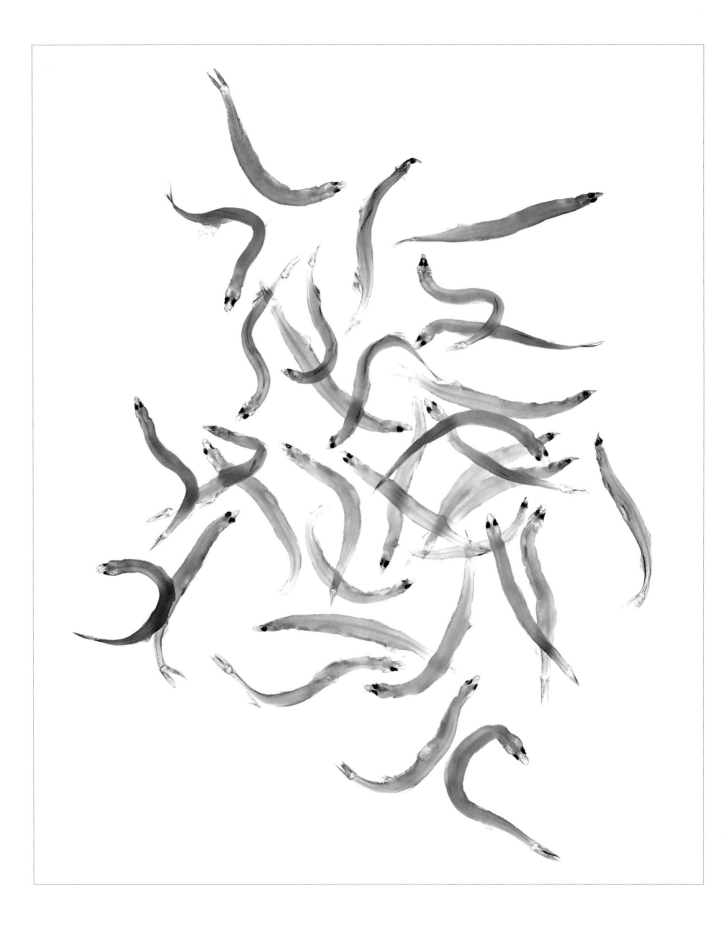

BIANCHETTI

*I*tty-bitty *bianchetti* are big in Sicily, where the locals go wild for the little larval offspring (or *neonata*) of the *pesce azzurro* category (anchovies, sardines, mackerel, and the like). Felidia chef and Sicilian native Fortunato Nicotra likes to toss them with linguine and cherry tomatoes, or to fry them up street-food style into fritters. Fresh *bianchetti* can be as hard to find stateside as they must be to catch, but they're worth seeking out at Italian specialty seafood shops. Randazzo's in the Bronx, for one, imports them from Greece, which is close enough to home for Nicotra.

Fortunato Nicotra's Frittelle di Bianchetti

2 egg whites

Sea salt

½ garlic clove, finely chopped

1 tablespoon finely chopped parsley

1 tablespoon finely chopped chives

1 tablespoon coarsely grated fresh
  pecorino cheese

1 tablespoon fresh bread
  crumbs or panko

1 cup fresh *bianchetti*

Grapeseed or olive oil

In a large bowl, gently beat the egg whites together with a pinch of salt until they start to turn foamy. Whisk in the garlic, herbs, pecorino, and bread crumbs. Add the *bianchetti* and gently stir to combine, making sure not to break the fish. (If the mixture appears a little watery, add more bread crumbs.) Coat the bottom of a large nonstick sauté pan with a ½- to ¾-inch layer of oil. Heat oil until very hot, between 325 and 340 degrees, but do not allow it to smoke. Using a tablespoon, scoop the *frittelle* mixture into loosely formed balls and add them to the hot oil, taking care not to overcrowd the pan. Cook for 2 to 3 minutes on each side, until golden brown. Place on paper towels to absorb excess oil, season to taste, and serve as is or with a spicy marinara sauce. ***Serves 4.***

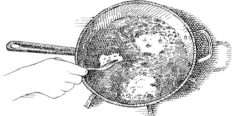

CELERY ROOT

Celery root, also known as celeriac, will never win any beauty contests. Although closely related to plain old celery, that staple of lunchboxes and dieters alike, the gnarly round root is mostly overlooked in this country, unlike in Italy and France, where it's turned into soups, purées, and that mayo-laden bistro staple, celeri rémoulade. At Mario Batali's Otto Enoteca Pizzeria, the odd knob is put to excellent seasonal use in a lively, citrus-laden winter salad. Cheese, of course, never hurts either.

Otto's Celery Root and Citrus Salad

1 Meyer lemon

2 blood oranges

1 Ruby Red grapefruit

1 pound (about 2 medium) celery roots

¼ cup tender inner celery leaves

¼ cup extra-virgin olive oil

1 tablespoon Champagne vinegar

Salt and freshly ground black pepper

4 ounces Parmigiano-Reggiano cheese,
    shaved with vegetable peeler

Peel and segment the citrus, squeezing and reserving the juice from whatever flesh remains on the membranes. Scrub roots, peel them with a sharp knife, and immerse them in a bowl of cold water and the reserved juice to prevent discoloration. Slice root into matchsticks using a mandoline. Toss slices with citrus segments, celery leaves, olive oil, vinegar, and salt and pepper to taste. Add half the cheese. Divide salad onto 4 plates and garnish with remaining cheese. *Serves 4.*

CHOCOLATE

Chocolate might always be in season, but never more so than in mid-February, when heart-shaped boxes beckon from every checkout line and love is calibrated in cacao content. One of the best expressions of the flavor can be found at the sleek Japanese dessert bar Kyotofu in New York, where the signature cupcake is enriched with soy milk, tofu, and just enough miso to give it a slight, delectable tang.

Kyotofu's Chocolate Soufflé Cupcakes

2 cups dark chocolate (preferably Valrhona pellets, 64 percent cacao)

8 tablespoons (1 stick) unsalted butter, softened

1 tablespoon white miso

3 eggs

¾ cup confectioners' sugar, plus more for dusting (optional)

¼ cup Japanese bread flour

¼ cup all-purpose flour

3½ teaspoons cocoa powder (preferably Valrhona)

1¼ teaspoons baking powder

¼ cup silken tofu

¼ cup soy milk, unsweetened (preferably Vitasoy)

Preheat oven to 325 degrees. Melt chocolate, butter, and miso in double boiler over low heat, stirring occasionally. When only small lumps remain, remove from heat and stir until completely smooth. Whip eggs and sugar until they double in volume and turn pale yellow in color. Pour chocolate mixture into mixing bowl with the eggs, varying the mixing speed to incorporate chocolate. Combine the remaining dry ingredients in a bowl, mixing together with hands or a whisk. Fold the dry ingredients into the chocolate, mixing until fully incorporated. Add tofu and soy milk slowly, mixing until fully incorporated. Scoop batter almost to the top of 24 wax-lined mini panettone cups arranged on a baking sheet. Bake for 20 minutes, rotating tray halfway through, until center springs back when touched. Dust with confectioners' sugar if desired. *Makes 24 cupcakes*.

CRAWFISH

With possibly more names than Eskimos have for snow, succulent Louisiana crawfish—aka mudbugs, yabbies, crayfish, crawdads, crawdaddies, creekcrabs, and *les écrevisses*—usually appear in late winter and are available through June. Call them whatever you want, but try them in this jambalaya riff from Joaquin Baca, a Texas expat, who opened Momofuku Noodle Bar with David Chang, and now provides New York with some of its best southern-style cooking at the Brooklyn Star in Williamsburg. Not only does he tell you how to cook a crawdad, but he shows you the proper way to eat one.

Joaquin Baca's Chicken, Sausage, and Crawfish Stew

2 to 3 tablespoons canola oil

4 chicken legs, drumsticks and thighs separated

1 pound andouille sausage, sliced on the bias about 1 inch thick

2 cups canned tomatoes, crushed

Salt to taste

Hot sauce to taste

1 tablespoon gumbo filé

3 pounds live crawfish

5 cups cooked white rice (should be a little undercooked; use about ½ cup less water than normal)

1 cup thinly sliced celery

Roughly torn celery leaves

2 tablespoons sliced scallion

1 tablespoon chopped parsley

In a large cast-iron pot, heat the oil over high heat. Add the chicken and sausage (in batches if the pot becomes too crowded) and brown until they achieve a nice even color, about 5 to 10 minutes. Add tomatoes and enough water to cover. Add salt and simmer for 45 minutes. If necessary, add more water to cover. Adjust seasoning. Add hot sauce to taste and filé powder. Add the crawfish, making sure they are submerged in the liquid. Cover pot and cook for 1 minute. Add the parcooked rice and simmer for about 5 minutes, until it has absorbed some liquid and the jambalaya isn't too soupy. Take pot off heat and add celery, celery leaves, scallion, and parsley. **Serves 5 to 7.**

HOW TO EAT A CRAWFISH

Twist the tail apart from the head. Peel away a bit of the top of the tail shell, and pinch tail just above the fans to get at the meat. Suck the juices from the head and scoop out the fat with your pinkie.

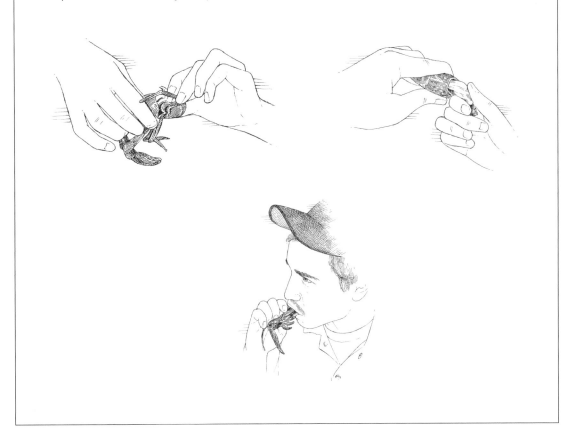

EMU EGGS

The next time you're in the market for a really jumbo-size egg, try the deep-green, pale-yolked ones laid by emus and increasingly sold at farmers' markets, including the one at New York's Union Square. Even though the fast but flightless birds are being raised locally, their laying schedule still conforms to the southern hemisphere, where they originally hail from. No less an egg maestro than WD-50's Wylie Dufresne brainstormed the perfect technique (oil poaching) to showcase the striking scale of the thing, without reducing it to a giant omelette.

Wylie Dufresne's Emu-Egg Fondue

1 emu egg

1 gallon grapeseed oil (or enough to
    cover egg suspended in a pot)

3 Yukon gold potatoes, cut into 1-inch
    cubes

Extra-virgin olive oil

Sea salt to taste

2 sprigs thyme

20 Brussels sprouts, cut in half or
    quarters

Sansho to season

20 breadsticks

16 strips cooked bacon

THE DAY BEFORE: Place the emu egg in a pasta basket that fits into a medium-size pot with high sides, and place the basket into the pot. Cover with oil until the egg is submerged. Remove the egg and the basket, then bring the oil up to 280 degrees. Place the egg and basket back in the oil and cover with a lid. Oil-poach the egg for 16 minutes, adjusting the heat as necessary to maintain a constant temperature. After 16 minutes, remove the basket and place egg into an ice bath to cool. Once cool, rinse the shell with soapy water to remove any remaining oil. Refrigerate overnight.

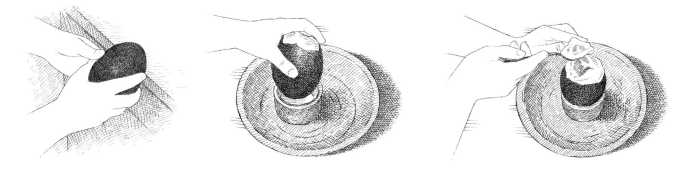

THE NEXT DAY: Preheat oven to 350 degrees. Toss the potatoes with the olive oil, salt, and thyme and place on a baking sheet in the oven for 20 minutes, turning occasionally. Toss the Brussels sprouts with olive oil and salt and add to the potatoes and cook for an additional 20 minutes, or until everything is nicely browned. Remove from oven and season to taste with *sansho*. While the vegetables are roasting, place the egg in a pot and cover with warm water. During the 20 minutes that the Brussels sprouts are roasting, reheat the egg over a low flame in the water at a temperature in which you may comfortably leave your finger for 3 seconds, approximately 160 degrees. (When done, the yolk should be liquidy but cooked, and the white should be solid.)

TO SERVE: Place the breadsticks, bacon, potatoes, and Brussels sprouts in serving dishes. Remove egg from water and pat dry. Carefully tap the egg on a counter edge, cracking the shell around the perimeter about 1½ inches from the top. Remove shell from the top, exposing the egg. Stand the egg in a roll of masking tape placed in a shallow bowl. Remove the exposed white to reveal the liquid yolk. For presentation, pour salt or arrange flowers or other decorative matter around and over the tape to hide it. Season the egg lightly with salt and *sansho*, and, using skewers, dip the breadsticks, bacon, and roasted vegetables into the yolk, as you would a fondue. Eat the remaining white with long sundae spoons. ***Serves 4 to 6.***

GERMAN BUTTERBALL POTATOES

A favorite among potato farmers, the German Butterball (no relation to the turkey) is an heirloom variety known as a "butterless" potato; because it's so good, you don't need butter. They store exceptionally well (which is why, although they're harvested in the fall, we've put them in the "Winter" section of this book), and possess a deep yellow flesh and a fairly dry and flaky texture. The nugget-size specimens available at farmers' markets are prized by chefs, like Annisa's Anita Lo, who appreciate the fact that the little spuds pack a ton of flavor into a small (and awfully cute) package. They're delicious simply steamed or mashed, but maybe even better stuffed with melted cheese, as in this riff on classic French raclette.

Anita Lo's German Butterballs with Raclette

12 small German Butterball potatoes

Kosher salt

⅔ cup grated raclette cheese

Optional garnishes: cornichons and chives, chopped; and
    prosciutto, sliced and chopped

Preheat oven to 450 degrees. Slice off about a quarter of the tops of each potato and a thin layer off the bottoms to form a solid base. Using a melon baller, scoop out the potatoes from the top to form small cups. Place the hollowed-out potatoes in a saucepan and cover with salted water. Bring to a boil, then simmer until the potatoes are tender, about 5 to 10 minutes. (You should be able to easily insert a knife into the thickest part of the potato.) Drain and cool. Stuff the cavities with the grated raclette, pressing down slightly. Place on a baking sheet and bake until cheese is melted and bubbly, about 5 minutes. Garnish as desired and serve immediately as an hors d'oeuvre, or pair with a small salad as an appetizer. ***Serves 4.***

HORSERADISH

Come January, it's slim pickings in Northeast farmers' markets, when devoted locavores are reduced to buying swollen tubers and gnarly, elongated roots, like the fresh horseradish that can typically be found all winter long. If you're accustomed to the stuff in a jar, the root looks almost primeval, like something that belongs in a witch's cauldron (and has, in fact, been used historically for medicinal and religious purposes). But its unique flavor—a piquant, biting sharpness with a sweet undertone—makes it a popular condiment and a zesty addition to the creamy dip Marc Meyer serves with bread at Cookshop.

Marc Meyer's Fresh Horseradish and Roasted-Onion Dip

1 small or half a medium-large
    horseradish root, peeled and diced
¼ cup white wine vinegar
Salt and freshly ground black pepper
    to taste

1 tablespoon olive oil
2 medium white onions, sliced
1 cup crème fraîche
1 teaspoon chopped fresh
    tarragon

Put horseradish, vinegar, and a pinch of salt in a food processor and pulse until smooth but not puréed. Reserve. Heat olive oil in a medium saucepan and add sliced onions. Cook over low flame until very soft, about 45 minutes. Let cool. In a food processor, pulse onions with pinch of salt and pepper until almost a purée. Remove from processor. Using a spatula, remove onion mixture from processor and combine with horseradish and crème fraîche until smooth. Fold in fresh tarragon. Serve with bread or breadsticks. *Serves 6.*

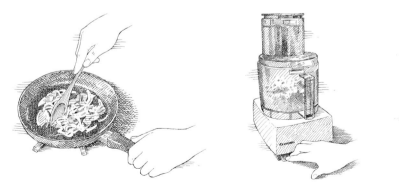

CALIFORNIA KIWIFRUIT

Although the fuzzy-skinned, egg-shaped kiwifruit is most closely associated with New Zealand, it was actually brought there from China in the early twentieth century. With its increase in popularity, New Zealanders renamed what they'd initially called the "Chinese gooseberry" after their national bird. Now, of course, it's grown elsewhere, too: the California crop is harvested in late fall, but stores so well it's readily available into spring (just as the New Zealand season kicks off, conveniently). Sweet-tart and juicy, the fruit is fairly bursting with all sorts of healthy substances, including vitamins C and E, potassium, and fiber, much of it in the edible skin. Michael Huynh, the peripatetic Vietnamese chef behind such Manhattan restaurants as Mai House and Baoguette, offers up this variation on the classic Vietnamese dipping sauce nuoc cham, which he serves with salt-and-pepper cuttlefish. It goes well with just about anything, though, especially grilled meats, chicken, and fish.

Michael Huynh's Sweet-and-Sour Kiwi Sauce

5 kiwifruits

1 Thai (or bird's-eye) chile

1 garlic clove, minced

Juice of 1 lime

1 tablespoon white wine vinegar

1 teaspoon fish sauce, or to taste

2 teaspoons sugar, or to taste, depending upon the sweetness of the kiwifruit

Freshly ground black pepper to taste

Cut the kiwifruit in half and scoop out the flesh. Purée the flesh and seeds in a blender or food processor and transfer to a bowl. Chop the chile and add to the purée along with remaining ingredients. Stir well to combine. *Makes about 1 cup.*

KUMQUATS

The kumquat is a bona fide Bizarro World citrus in that its peel is sweet and its flesh tart. And you can eat the eccentric little buggers whole—skin, seeds, and all. Just pop one in your mouth like an M&M and see. And kumquats go well with cognac—"the most kumquat-y" spirit out there, according to PDT's Jim Meehan, who provides potable proof.

Jim Meehan's Kumquat Cobbler

3 kumquats

> 1½ ounces Pierre Ferrand Ambre cognac
> ½ ounce Strega liqueur
> ½ ounce fresh lemon juice
> ¼ ounce Lemon Hart 151 Demerara rum
> ¼ ounce simple syrup
> Half a lemon wheel, for garnish

Slice a thin wheel from the center of one of the kumquats and reserve. Muddle the kumquats, then add to a cocktail shaker with the cognac, liqueur, lemon juice, rum, and simple syrup. Shake with ice cubes and strain into a Collins glass filled with crushed or pebble ice. Garnish with kumquat wheel attached to half lemon wheel with a cocktail pick. *Makes 1 drink.*

LOTUS ROOT

Lotus root, the crisp, mildly sweet aquatic plant that's ubiquitous in stir-fries and fried into chips, can be readily found at Asian groceries from fall through late winter. It has traditional significance, though, on Chinese New Year, as it's said to allow new ventures to take root and grow. Annisa chef Anita Lo has served it as dessert on a special holiday menu, stuffing the root's characteristic holes with lotus-seed purée. Here she shares a simplified version of her recipe, which should bring home cooks good luck any time of year.

Anita Lo's Lotus Root with Lotus Seeds

2 segments lotus root

2 cups sugar

½ teaspoon salt, plus a pinch

1 cup dried lotus seeds

¼ vanilla bean, split and scraped

1 tablespoon fresh lemon juice

Peel and remove ends of lotus root. Place roots and sugar in a small, deep pot with a pinch of salt and 2½ cups of water to cover. Bring to a boil, then simmer 10 to 15 minutes, or until roots are soft but slightly crunchy. Let cool. Split the dried lotus seeds and discard the bitter green centers. Place the cleaned lotus seeds in a separate pot with water to cover. Bring to a boil and simmer until very soft, about 15 to 20 minutes. Drain, then purée in a food processor with vanilla, ½ teaspoon salt, and a little of the lotus-root cooking liquid, adding more liquid as needed to achieve a very smooth, pipable consistency. Transfer to a pastry bag fitted with a small round tip and pipe into lotus-root holes, then chill the roots and the cooking liquid. To serve, add lemon juice to cooking liquid, slice roots into rounds, and drizzle with cooking liquid. ***Serves 4 to 6.***

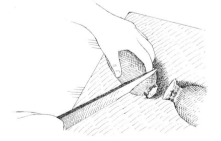

MEYER LEMON

*I*f you were going to go and have a lemon named after you, you could do a lot worse than the Meyer. Sweeter, richer, and rounder (in both shape and flavor) than a regular lemon, it bears the name of USDA scout Frank N. Meyer, who lugged the citrus back from a trip he took to Beijing in 1908. Widely grown in California, the smooth-skinned fruit is a cross between a lemon and a mandarin, and you can substitute it for its common cousin in any number of recipes. A cool pitcher of Meyer lemonade on a blistering hot day is a glorious thing. And in the thick of winter, when citrus fruit is at its best, a Meyer lemon adds a welcome note of brightness to just about anything it comes in contact with, including Roman-born New York chef Sandro Fioriti's signature pasta dish, spaghettini *al limone*.

Sandro Fioriti's Spaghettini al Limone

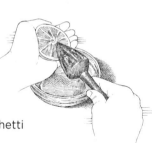

1 Meyer lemon

2 ounces unsalted butter

Freshly ground white pepper

Pinch of salt

1 pint heavy cream

1 pound spaghettini or spaghetti

¼ cup freshly grated
  Parmigiano-Reggiano cheese

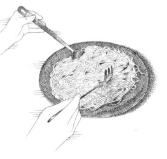

Zest and juice the Meyer lemon. Heat the butter in a sauté pan. Add Meyer lemon juice (pulp and seeds strained), zest, white pepper, and salt. When butter is melted and the mixture starts to boil, add cream, and the moment it returns to a boil remove pan from heat. Cook pasta al dente in salted water. Return sauce to burner and bring to a boil. Drain spaghetti and toss with sauce in the pan. Remove from heat and stir in the grated cheese. *Serves 4.*

MUSSELS

Not only are mussels a great bargain, but according to seafood scholar Taras Grescoe, they "clean the oceans and reduce the size of dead zones." In his book *Bottomfeeder: How to Eat Ethically in a World of Vanishing Seafood*, he categorizes the shellfish as one worth tucking into "absolutely, always." Aside from environmental advantages, mussels function as a bit of a blank (if delicious) canvas for creative chefs like Tien Ho, who recently ran the kitchen at Má Pêche in midtown Manhattan. Mussels are best in the winter months, when they're particularly sweet and plump. Look for ones whose shells are tightly closed or those that snap shut when given a tap (indicating they're still alive), and pass on any that are wide open.

Má Pêche's Mussels in Crab-Paste Beer Broth

FOR THE CRAB-PASTE BROTH

10 garlic cloves,
    roughly chopped

5 shallots, chopped

¼ cup canola oil

¼ cup crab paste

1½ teaspoons shrimp paste

Pinch of chile flakes

½ cup beer

FOR THE PICKLED BEAN SPROUTS

¼ cup vinegar

¼ cup water

1 tablespoon sugar

¼ pound bean sprouts

FOR THE MUSSELS

2 pounds mussels

2 tablespoons unsalted butter

1¼ cups beer

1 bunch Vietnamese mint, stemmed
    and chopped

Fish sauce to taste

FOR THE CRAB-PASTE BROTH: In a medium-size pan over medium heat, cook the garlic and shallots in the canola oil until fragrant, about 4 minutes. Add the crab paste, shrimp paste, and chile flakes, and cook for 4 more minutes. Add the beer and mix. Remove from heat and reserve.

FOR THE PICKLED BEAN SPROUTS: In a small pot, bring rice vinegar, water, and sugar to a boil and pour over bean sprouts. Let cool and reserve.

FOR THE MUSSELS: Clean the mussels well under cold running water and remove any "beards," the fibrous tufts protruding from shells. In a medium pot, over high heat, add the mussels, the reserved crabpaste broth, butter, and beer. Cover, and cook until mussels begin to open. Remove from heat and add reserved pickled bean sprouts and mint, and stir. Season with fish sauce. *Serves 2*.

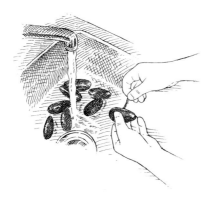

NORTHERN SPY APPLES

A late bloomer and, sadly, a bit of a rarity these days, the Northern Spy is considered a winter apple, ready for picking in October or November, with a sweet-tart flavor that only gets better in storage. It's a particular favorite among apple-pie bakers (when cooked, the slices hold their shape) and out-of-hand chompers alike. Liza Queen, the chef-owner of Potlikker restaurant in Williamsburg, Brooklyn, is a big fan. "If I had to conjure up the epitome of appleness," she says, "it would be the Northern Spy."

Liza Queen's Roasted Northern Spy Apples

2 large Northern Spy
　apples
Half a lemon
1 small poblano pepper

2 strips good bacon
2 large sage leaves
1 tablespoon extra-virgin olive oil
¼ teaspoon freshly ground black pepper

Preheat oven to 350 degrees. Cut apples in half. With a spoon or melon baller, core out seeded part only, and place apples on baking sheet flesh side up. Squeeze lemon over apples. Halve and deseed poblano pepper and julienne as thinly as possible. Cut bacon and sage leaves into thin julienned strips. Scatter the strips of poblano, bacon, and sage leaves over apples. Drizzle with the olive oil and season with the black pepper. Place sheet on middle oven rack and roast for 30 to 40 minutes, until soft, depending on the size of the apples. Serve as is with roast pork, or cooled and sliced in a salad, or as an appetizer with good Cheddar. *Serves 4.*

NEW-HARVEST OLIVE OIL

There are people who await each year's arrival of fresh-off-the-presses extra-virgin olive oil as if it were the first white truffle. Frank Castronovo and Frank Falcinelli of Frankies Spuntino are two such *olio nuovo* connoisseurs. They have their own organic, unfiltered house brand pressed and bottled in Sicily, and once the new shipment lands, they use the vibrant elixir in everything. When stocking up, check the bottle for the harvest date, and when you find a variety you like, don't hoard it. Lap it up, in salad dressings, with crusty bread and raw vegetables, and in recipes such as this ultraquick pasta, before its ephemeral freshness begins to fade.

Frankies Spuntino's Orecchiette with Horseradish and Parmesan

1 pound orecchiette

Kosher salt

4 ounces fresh horseradish

3 ounces (6 tablespoons) *olio nuovo,* or
    new-harvest olive oil

½ cup tomato sauce

Pinch of crushed red pepper flakes

6 ounces Parmigiano-Reggiano cheese,
    freshly grated

Parsley, for garnish

Cook pasta in salted water. While it's cooking, grate horseradish. When the pasta is cooked al dente, reserve 4 to 6 ounces of pasta water, then drain and place pasta in a sauté pan over low to medium heat. Add the reserved water in stages and add the olive oil, tomato sauce, and crushed red pepper, tossing the pan all the while (the entire process should take only a couple of minutes). Remove pan from heat and add the horseradish, cheese, and parsley with one last toss. **Serves 4 to 6**.

PARSNIPS

Although it does a fairly good imitation of a carrot, do not attempt to eat a parsnip in its natural state. Nature designed this cream-colored root for cooking. Roasting and frying in particular—both demonstrated in a single Thomas Keller recipe, below—bring out the winter vegetable's sweet and mellow flavor.

Bouchon Bakery's Roasted-Parsnip Salad

5 medium parsnips, plus 2 for frying

10 tablespoons (1¼ sticks) unsalted butter

½ cup honey

Salt and freshly ground black pepper to taste

1 orange, zested and sectioned

1 star anise, ground

Canola oil, for frying

1 head frisée, cleaned and dried, leaves separated

1 teaspoon chopped chives

1 teaspoon minced shallot

1 teaspoon lemon juice

1 teaspoon olive oil

Grapefruit marmalade (below; optional)

FOR THE ROASTED PARSNIPS: Preheat oven to 400 degrees. Peel the 5 parsnips and cut into baton shape. In a small pan, melt butter. In a bowl, toss the parsnips with honey, melted butter, and salt. Place parsnips in shallow baking pan and bake in oven until tender, about 20 minutes. Remove from oven and return parsnips to bowl. Fold in orange zest and ground star anise. Set aside.

FOR THE FRIED PARSNIPS: Peel and clean the remaining 2 parsnips. Using a vegetable peeler, slice the parsnips into thin ribbons. In a deep frying pan, heat the canola oil to 300 degrees. Fry the parsnip ribbons in batches until golden brown, remove to paper towels, and season with salt and pepper.

TO ASSEMBLE SALAD: Toss frisée with chives, shallot, lemon juice, and olive oil. Season with salt and pepper. Place the roasted parsnips on the plate. Place the frisée salad in a mound in the middle of the plate and top with the fried parsnip ribbons. Garnish with orange segments and a swirl of grapefruit marmalade if desired. ***Serves 4.***

Grapefruit Marmalade

3 grapefruits

1 cup grapefruit juice

1 cup Champagne vinegar

1 cup sugar

Water

Zest grapefruit and reserve the zest. Using a vegetable peeler, peel grapefruit and then dice the peel. Place in pot and cover with cold water. Bring to a boil and strain. Repeat two more times. Strain and reserve. Combine grapefruit juice, Champagne vinegar, sugar, and ½ cup water and bring to a boil. Add zest and cook over low heat until thickened. Let cool to room temperature.

PERSIMMONS

No fruit—or berry, if you want to get technical—demonstrates the virtue of patience more dramatically than the persimmon. So mouth-furringly astringent is the unripened Hachiya variety, it's barely edible. But wait until it's as soft as custard and you'll swear there is no fruit more perfectly sweet, more luxuriously fleshed, more subtly sophisticated. If you're the impatient sort, go for the shorter, squatter Fuyu variety, firm when ripe and a lot less tannic. Conventional wisdom dictates that Fuyus are for salads and Hachiyas for puréeing and steamed puddings, but either one works nicely in this recipe from Elizabeth Benno, who created it for Eataly's Le Verdure restaurant.

Elizabeth Benno's Grilled Persimmon Bruschetta

½ cup (4 ounces) fresh goat cheese

3 tablespoons extra-virgin olive oil

Salt and freshly ground black pepper
   to taste

2 tablespoons chopped parsley

1 nearly ripe Hachiya persimmon (or 2
   Fuyu persimmons)

2 slices of rustic white bread, cut
   1 inch thick

1 garlic clove, halved

In a small bowl, combine the cheese, 1 tablespoon of olive oil, and salt and pepper to taste. Mix in the parsley and reserve. Cut off the stem end of the persimmon and slice the fruit into wedges. Season with olive oil, salt, and pepper. Place on grill over medium heat and char the slices on both sides. Reserve. Drizzle the bread with olive oil and season with salt and pepper, then grill both sides. Remove from grill and rub one side of each slice of bread with garlic. Spread goat-cheese mixture over each slice and top with grilled persimmon. ***Serves 2.***

PINK GRAPEFRUIT

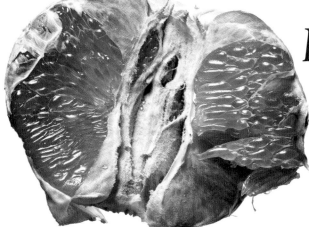

*F*or some, grapefruit season means making your way through a Florida gift box, one perfunctory breakfast at a time. For Dirt Candy chef/owner Amanda Cohen, it means this dressed-up winter salad that calls for more than simple sliced segments. She candies them instead (because "Who doesn't like candy in a salad?"), embellishing mixed greens with grapefruit "pops" and grilled cheese "croutons."

Amanda Cohen's Grapefruit Salad

GRAPEFRUIT

8 pink grapefruit segments with peel and pith removed but membrane attached

3 cups sugar

½ cup water

DRESSING

¼ cup grapefruit juice

2 tablespoons grapefruit zest

2 tablespoons lemon juice

1 tablespoon finely minced shallot

½ teaspoon Dijon mustard

2 teaspoons salt, plus more to taste

¼ teaspoon freshly ground black pepper, plus more to taste

¾ cup extra-virgin olive oil

SALAD

4 cups mixed greens

¼ ripe avocado, cubed

3 tablespoons toasted sliced almonds

CROUTONS

1 grilled cheese sandwich

FOR GRAPEFRUIT: Push an 8-inch-long bamboo skewer vertically about halfway through each segment. In a heavy stockpot over medium heat, bring the sugar and water to 385 degrees, until the liquid turns medium amber, and turn off heat. Tilt the pot, and very carefully dip each segment in the hot sugar to coat thoroughly, letting the excess drip off in the pot. Stick the skewers at an angle into a foil-wrapped piece of foam (floral or heavy Styrofoam), and let the grapefruit harden.

FOR DRESSING: In a blender mix everything but the oil, then slowly stream it in. Season with salt and pepper to taste.

FOR CROUTONS: Make a grilled cheese sandwich to your liking (Cohen uses 5 Spoke Creamery's Tumbleweed cheese and Sullivan St Bakery's *filone*). Cut sandwich into quarters, then slice each quarter diagonally.

FOR SALAD: Mix the greens with the dressing, toss in the avocado and almonds, and divide among 4 plates. Garnish each with 2 grapefruit pops and 2 croutons. *Serves 4.*

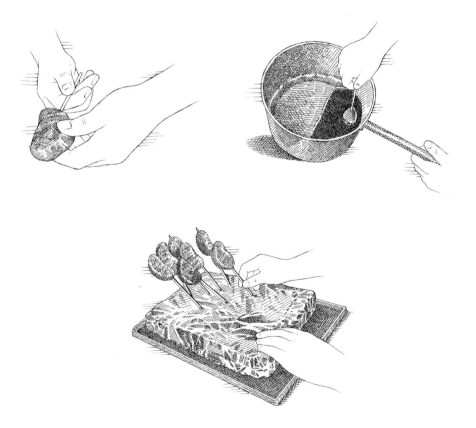

POMELO

A bit of a false advertiser, the pomelo—aka pummelo, aka pimplenose, aka citrus maxima—looks like it could easily deliver a gallon of juice for breakfast, with plenty left over to top off a round of pomelo Bellinis for brunch. But much of this hefty fruit's bulk belongs to a thick pith that looks and feels a little like Owens Corning Fiberglas insulation. Nevertheless, the bigger the fruit, the more rind there is to candy. Patricia Yeo shared her recipe for the bittersweet treat when she was chef of New York's Sapa, before moving on to cook in Boston and compete on *Top Chef Masters*.

Patricia Yeo's Candied Pomelo Peel

1 large pomelo

Water

2 cups sugar, plus more for tossing

Milk chocolate (optional)

Peel pomelo, taking care to remove as much of the pith as possible, and reserve fruit for another use. Cut the peel into ¼-inch-wide strips. Fill a small pot with water and bring to a boil. Add the pomelo peel and blanch for 1 minute. Remove peel and drain. Repeat three times, changing water each time (this removes some of the peel's bitterness). After the third blanching, refill pot with 2 cups fresh water and 2 cups sugar. Dissolve sugar over medium-low heat. Bring to a boil, add the peel back to the pot, and reduce heat to low. Cook until the peel is translucent and almost no liquid remains, about 1 hour. Remove the peel from the pot and cool on a wire rack. Toss in sugar or dip in melted chocolate. Store in airtight container for up to one week.

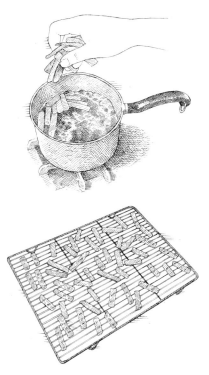

REDBOR KALE

This fantas- tically frilly but superhardy hybrid kale comes in a magnificent shade of Crayola magenta (or is it fuchsia?) and is grown as often for ornamental purposes as it is for eating. But don't let that stop you from tossing it into a salad, like the one from New York's Northern Spy Food Co. (Its former chef Nathan Foot typically used the crinkly-leafed *cavolo nero* variety, but his method applies just as well to other types.) It's funny to think that, not so long ago, offering a pile of raw kale to the general dining public was tantamount to offering them a bale of hay. Not so these kale-crazed days. The trick is cutting the leaves into thin strips and hand-mixing them vigorously with olive oil, salt, and lemon juice as if you were shampooing a Labradoodle, which has a delicious tenderizing effect.

Nathan Foot's Kale Salad

2½ cups Redbor kale

1 tablespoon lemon juice

2 tablespoons extra-virgin olive oil

Salt and freshly ground black
  pepper to taste

¼ cup toasted almonds, halved

¼ cup crumbled Cabot clothbound
  Cheddar cheese (or any good-
  quality, well-aged Cheddar)

½ cup cubed, seasoned, and roasted
  kabocha squash

Pecorino Romano cheese to taste

Cut off the bottom stems from the kale and discard. Remove stems from the individual leaves by folding each leaf in half and cutting away the stem at the fold. Stack several stemmed leaves together at a time, roll stack into a tight cylinder, and slice the cylinder crosswise at ¼-inch intervals. Put the resulting kale strips in a large mixing bowl. Add the lemon juice and olive oil. Season with salt and pepper and, using your hands, mix well. Mix in the almonds, Cheddar, and squash. Divide salad onto 2 plates. Finely grate pecorino over each portion. ***Serves 2.***

RED CABBAGE

Cabbage comes by its bad rep by being boiled to within an inch of its life. That, thankfully, is not the only way to treat this wonderfully crisp vegetable, whose hardiness makes it a cold-weather staple wherever it grows. With more vitamin C than its green and Savoy brethren, red cabbage is particularly invaluable during winter, when good fresh salads, like the apple-and-walnut–strewn one Kurt Gutenbrunner serves at Blaue Gans, are few and far between.

Kurt Gutenbrunner's Red Cabbage Salad

2 tablespoons sherry vinegar
2 tablespoons walnut oil
1 tablespoon lingonberry jam
1 teaspoon sugar
½ head red cabbage

2 apples
½ teaspoon fresh lemon juice
1 cup walnuts, toasted and chopped
Salt and freshly ground black pepper

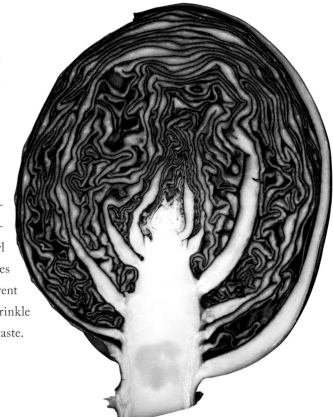

In a large mixing bowl, combine sherry vinegar, walnut oil, lingonberry jam, and sugar. Using a mandoline or a knife, slice cabbage very thin. Add to bowl and toss. Slice apples into thin disks. Lay 5 apple slices on each plate and sprinkle with lemon juice to prevent discoloration. Top with red cabbage mixture and sprinkle with walnuts. Season with salt and pepper to taste. ***Serves 4 to 6.***

RUTABAGA

*I*ts parents were a cabbage and a turnip. The French do not like them and consider them fodder. The Russians have a saying, loosely translated: "I'm as sick of you as of rutabaga." And in Ithaca, they use them instead of stones to play the sport of curling. Still, the plant has hidden depths; beneath its gnarly exterior there lies a lovely golden flesh, a certain sweetness, and an appealing starchiness that takes well to mashing with butter—a technique deftly applied by Spotted Pig alum Nate Smith, the chef of Brooklyn gastropub Allswell.

Nate Smith's Smashed Rutabagas and Carrots

2 medium rutabagas

5 medium carrots

8 tablespoons (1 stick) butter

1 teaspoon sugar

2 teaspoons salt

Pinch of ground chile flakes

1 sprig tarragon

1 cup water

1 tablespoon roughly chopped flat-leaf
  parsley

Slice the ends off the rutabagas, peel, and cut into large dice. Peel the carrots and cut into large dice. Place all of the ingredients except water and parsley in a saucepan and add the water until it reaches halfway up the diced vegetables. Cover with a parchment lid and cook over medium heat, adding more water if necessary, until the vegetables are soft enough to mash and the water has been absorbed. Remove tarragon and roughly mash the rutabaga-carrot mixture using a potato masher. Adjust seasoning. Sprinkle with chopped parsley. *Serves 4.*

SAVOY CABBAGE

Say what you will about the English and their cuisine, their flair for naming dishes is unsurpassed. Take, for instance, bubble and squeak: an ideal cold-weather application of cabbage, one of the market's few late-season holdouts. The name, it's said, evokes either the sweet sound of the stuff cooking in the skillet, or—depending on the talent of the cook—that of a gurgling, postprandial stomach. Our gurgle-free version comes from the Spotted Pig's April Bloomfield, who prefers the crinkly, wrinkly (and squeakier, perhaps?) Savoy variety for its crisper leaf and mellower flavor.

April Bloomfield's Bubble and Squeak

1 pound Savoy cabbage

1 medium yellow onion, thinly sliced

8 tablespoons (1 stick) plus 2 tablespoons
　　unsalted butter

Maldon sea salt and freshly ground black pepper to taste

½ pound Brussels sprouts, outer layer removed and thinly sliced

1 pound Yukon Gold potatoes, peeled and cut in half

4 eggs, for frying

Preheat oven to 400 degrees. Thinly slice cabbage. In large stainless-steel pan, sweat onions in 4 tablespoons of butter and a pinch of salt over medium heat for 5 to 10 minutes, until soft. Add cabbage and Brussels sprouts and cook for an additional 15 minutes. Meanwhile, in a saucepan, boil potatoes in salted water until tender. Drain potatoes and thoroughly dry, letting all the steam evaporate. Return potatoes to the saucepan, add 2 tablespoons of butter, and mash with a hand masher. Add cabbage mixture to potatoes, adjust seasoning, and mold by hand into 4 patties. Heat 1 tablespoon of butter in each of 4 nonstick blini pans and cook over burner until frothy, then brown patties in pans for 2 to 3 minutes. Bake patties in pans in oven for 15 minutes, then flip into plates and serve with fried eggs. **Serves 4.**

TRIPE

If you've never tried tripe, New Year's Day presents the perfect opportunity. That's the traditional time to eat *menudo*, the spicy tripe stew that's said to banish hangovers. Julie E. Farias, the chef of Goat Town in New York, grew up on the stuff in San Antonio, Texas, where her family sells it at their meat market. She recommends serving it with some ice-cold Reissdorf Kölsch in the role of hair of the dog.

Julie E. Farias's Menudo

5 pounds honeycomb tripe, cleaned

1 small yellow onion, peeled

1 lemon

1 head of garlic, top trimmed

Half of a calf's foot (ask to have it cut horizontally into approximately 1½-inch pieces)

¼ cup chile powder, or more for a spicier taste or darker color

1½ tablespoons salt, or to taste

½ tablespoon garlic powder

½ tablespoon onion powder

1½ tablespoons dried oregano

2 (30-ounce) cans hominy, drained

FOR GARNISH

White onion, chopped

8 to 10 lemon wedges

Cilantro

Corn tortillas, warmed

Cut tripe into large pieces, then into thin strips. Prick yellow onion, lemon, and garlic with a fork several times, then wrap them in cheesecloth with the calf's foot and tie with twine. Put in a large soup or stock pot and cover with 6 quarts of water. Bring to a boil, then add tripe. Reduce heat and simmer, stirring occasionally and skimming the surface scum but leaving the layer of fat. After 3 hours, add spices and hominy. Add more water to cover if necessary and adjust seasoning to taste. Simmer for 1 more hour, until the tripe shrivels up and develops a gelatinous texture. Remove cheesecloth. Serve *menudo* in bowls garnished with white onion, a wedge of lemon, and a sprig of cilantro, and warm tortillas on the side. **Serves 8 to 10.**

VACHERIN MONT D'OR

As eagerly anticipated among its fervent followers as Christmas Day is among the townsfolk of Whoville, Vacherin Mont d'Or is a truly seasonal cheese, made from the autumn and winter milk of the same speckled Swiss cows that give us Swiss Gruyère. Unless you smuggle the raw-milk, aged-for-less-than-sixty-days variety past Customs, you'll have to settle for a *fromage* made from milk that's been thermized (like pasteurization-lite). Still, when perfectly ripe and properly oozing, it's a fairly spectacular thing with a relentless barnyard-y aroma. Eat it with a spoon from its sprucewood container with some fruit and nuts, or wrap it in foil, box and all, and pop it in the oven for a no-cleanup-required fondue.

Baked Vacherin

One (1-pound) wheel of Vacherin Mont d'Or
2 or 3 garlic cloves
Splash or two of white wine

Preheat oven to 375 degrees. Discard the box lid and prick the top of the cheese's rind a few times with a knife. Insert garlic cloves into the cheese, and drizzle the wine over the top. Wrap the cheese (still in its box bottom) in a piece of aluminum foil, leaving the top open. Place in oven and bake for approximately 20 minutes, until oozing. Serve hot with crusty bread for dipping and cornichons, or spooned over boiled potatoes. *Serves 4.*

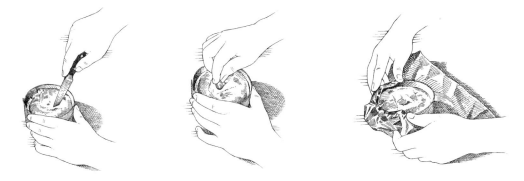

CAVOLO NERO

Like dandelion greens and zucchini blossoms, *cavolo nero* (aka black kale) is one of those beautiful old-time plants once categorized as peasant fare and now, of course, all the rage among today's *cucina povera* foodies. Like other kales, it positively thrives in cold weather and its blue-black bubble-wrap texture and slightly bitter flavor only improve after the first frost. Cut the raw leaves into ribbons and dress them with lemon, olive oil, garlic, and grated pecorino, and you have a wonderful—if slightly chewy—winter salad. For something on the complete opposite end of the texture spectrum, try this soul-soothing recipe from Cesare Casella, the chef of New York's Salumeria Rosi and the dean of Italian Studies at the International Culinary Center, who, in the Italian manner, favors cooking the bouncy leaves until they're almost unrecognizably soft and tender.

Cesare Casella's Cavolo Nero *Bruschetta*

1 pound *cavolo nero*

¼ cup extra-virgin olive oil

6 garlic cloves, sliced, plus 1 whole clove

2 teaspoons dried red pepper flakes

Salt and freshly ground black pepper to taste

1 quart vegetable stock or water

1½ cups canned peeled tomatoes with juice

4 large slices of rustic Italian bread

Wash kale and remove any hard stems by folding leaves in half lengthwise and cutting or pulling the stem away from the leaves. Slice or tear leaves into 1-inch pieces. Heat olive oil and sliced garlic in a large skillet over medium heat. When the garlic turns golden brown, add the red pepper flakes, kale, salt, and pepper and cook for approximately 30 minutes. Add the vegetable stock or water and tomatoes with juice and cook for approximately 15 minutes, stirring continuously, until the mixture is reduced. Toast the bread and rub each slice with the remaining clove of garlic. Place mixture on toast and serve as is or with a sunny-side-up egg on top of each slice. *Serves 4.*

BLACK-EYED PEAS

D espite their year-round availability, dried black-eyed peas get their chance to shine in the form of hoppin' John, a southern specialty believed to bring good luck when eaten on New Year's Day. Traditionally prepared with smoked pork and white rice, the dish is open to creative interpretation—like this Italianized version from native New Yorker Bobby Flay.

Bobby Flay's Hoppin' John Risotto

½ pound dried black-eyed peas

1 pound applewood-smoked slab bacon

6 sprigs fresh thyme, plus 1 tablespoon finely chopped fresh thyme, for garnish

Salt and freshly ground black pepper

6 cups homemade chicken stock or low-sodium canned chicken broth

2 tablespoons olive oil

1 medium Spanish onion, finely chopped

1 garlic clove, finely chopped

1½ cups Arborio rice

1 cup dry white wine

Pick over the peas to remove dirt and stones. Soak them in water to cover at least 4 hours or overnight. Drain the peas and transfer to a medium saucepan. Cover with fresh water. Cut the slab of bacon in half crosswise and add one of the halves to the saucepan along with the thyme sprigs. Bring to a boil over high heat, reduce the heat to medium, and simmer until tender, 45 to 60 minutes. Season with salt and pepper. Drain the peas, transfer to a bowl, and remove the bacon and thyme sprigs. Cut the remaining half of bacon into small dice. Place the bacon in a medium sauté pan over medium heat and cook until golden brown and crisp. Remove the bacon with a slotted spoon and transfer to a plate lined with paper towels. Bring the stock to a simmer over low heat in a large saucepan. Heat the oil in a large saucepan over high heat. Add the onions and cook until soft, 3 to 4 minutes. Add the garlic and cook for 30 seconds. Stir in the rice and cook for 2 minutes, until lightly toasted and opaque. Add the wine and cook until completely reduced. Add 2 cups of the hot stock and cook, stirring, until evaporated. Repeat with the remaining stock, adding 1 cup at a time until the rice is al dente, 20 to 25 minutes. Stir in the black-eyed peas and chopped thyme and season with salt and pepper. Transfer the risotto to a large shallow bowl and top with the crispy bacon. *Serves 4 to 6.*

WINTER GREENS

Though not as easy and accessible as their delicate summer counterparts, winter greens, or "cooking greens," have their own assertive allure—not to mention an abundance of vitamins, minerals, and fiber. The darker the green, the better, nutritionally speaking, but each has its distinctive, sometimes bracingly bitter flavor. At Lassi, the Indian takeout spot she opened as an unexpected digresssion in a pastry-chef career, Heather Carlucci-Rodriguez seasoned them with hot chile, ginger, and the caramelized sweetness of roasted baby Brussels sprouts.

Heather Carlucci-Rodriguez's Braised Greens with Roasted Baby Brussels Sprouts

1 pound baby Brussels sprouts, cleaned

1 tablespoon kosher salt

2 tablespoons canola oil

½ teaspoon *chaat masala*

1 tablespoon peeled, grated fresh ginger

2 Thai chiles, minced

2 pounds braising greens, thoroughly washed, stems removed (kale, Swiss chard, mustard greens, beet greens, turnip greens)

Salt and freshly ground black pepper to taste

TO PREPARE BRUSSELS SPROUTS: Preheat oven to 400 degrees. Toss sprouts with kosher salt, 1 tablespoon canola oil, and *chaat masala*. Turn out onto sheet pan or rimmed cookie sheet and roast for 25 to 30 minutes or until slightly charred and tender.

TO PREPARE GREENS: Heat remaining oil in a deep sauté pan. Add ginger and chiles. Cook for 1 minute. Add greens and 1 cup water. Cover and cook over low heat for 5 to 7 minutes, until greens are dark and wilted. Season with salt and pepper and combine with Brussels sprouts. *Serves 4.*

BLACK RADISH

To connoisseurs of the elegant breakfast radish, the pale and lovely icicle variety, or their psychedelic watermelon kin, the black radish comes off as bulbous and clunky. But this particular specimen lasts longer than most; possesses drier flesh and a spicier, more pungent bite; and is reputed, among holistic types, to cure what ails you in the digestive and respiratory departments. It tastes great raw, with a sprinkle of salt, or grated into soups. Chef Neil Ferguson, the opening chef for Gordon Ramsay at The London in New York, tempers the root's characteristic bite in a rich, creamy gratin.

Neil Ferguson's Black Radish Gratin

1 pound black radishes

1 cup heavy cream

1 cup milk

2 tablespoons butter

1 garlic clove, crushed

1 sprig fresh thyme

1 bay leaf

Pinch of nutmeg

Salt and freshly ground black pepper

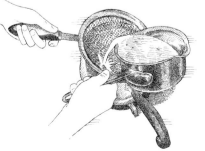

Preheat oven to 350 degrees. Peel radishes and slice them very thin (¹⁄₁₆ of an inch if possible) on a mandoline. In a saucepan, combine the remaining ingredients. Bring to a simmer, then turn off heat and allow to infuse for about 10 minutes. Strain cream mixture into another saucepan, discarding solids. Add sliced radishes and simmer over medium heat for about 5 minutes. Remove from heat. Remove radish slices with a perforated spoon, and layer them in a small casserole. Cover with cream mixture and bake for about 30 minutes, or until golden and bubbly, and serve with roast leg of lamb, pork, or veal chop. *Serves 4.*

CARA CARA ORANGES

*I*n the middle of winter-citrus season, we often find ourselves looking for something else to do with our weekly haul than eat it for breakfast. One intoxicating option: this cocktailian take on the screwdriver that dusts off the old relic by employing bitters and an Italian citrus liqueur. Most crucial is the inclusion of freshly squeezed juice from clementines and Cara Cara oranges, the pinkish-red navels known for their subtle berry flavor.

No. 7 Sub's Screwdriver

1 Cara Cara orange

1 clementine

1½ ounces Tito's Handmade Vodka

½ ounce Nardini Acqua di Cedro

1 dash Regan's Orange Bitters

4 dashes Peychaud's Bitters

Juice Cara Cara orange and clementine. Combine in a cocktail shaker with the remaining ingredients and ice, and shake. Strain into an ice-filled rocks or highball glass. ***Makes 1 drink.***

EELS

Back in Colonial days, eels were as popular with the locals as three-cornered hats and buckle shoes. Not so today, except among sushiphiles. Eels do have their moment, though, at Christmastime, when Italian-Americans seek them out for the traditional Christmas Eve dinner known as La Vigilia, or Feast of the Seven Fishes. Sicilian-born chef Fortunato Nicotra, who runs the kitchen at Lidia Bastianich's Felidia restaurant on Manhattan's East Side, throws as good an eel-centric Vigilia as anyone. He prizes the snake-like fish for its sweet, rich flavor and uses it in a slew of recipes. You can find eels—skinned and filleted and ready to throw into the pot—at any good fishmonger's. Thrill seekers might want to look for them at farmers' markets, where the squirmy things are sometimes sold live.

Fortunato Nicotra's *Eel* alla Veneziana

1 large sweet onion, sliced

3 bay leaves

2 tablespoons extra-virgin olive oil

1 pound fresh eel, cleaned and skinned

Sea salt to taste

Freshly ground black pepper to taste

2 tablespoons red wine vinegar

Polenta, prepared

In a large nonstick pan, sauté the sliced onion and bay leaves in olive oil for approximately 5 minutes, until the onions color slightly. Cut the eel into 1-inch pieces, season with salt and pepper, and add to the pan. Cover and cook for 5 more minutes, shaking the pan occasionally. Remove lid, and deglaze the pan with red wine vinegar, allowing the vinegar to evaporate. Adjust seasoning and serve over polenta. *Makes 4 appetizer-size portions.*

COLLARD GREENS

Winter is the time when collards come into their own, their big, bouncy, olive-green leaves fairly bursting with all sorts of vitamins and minerals. Harlem's reigning soul food king, Charles Gabriel of Charles' Pan-Fried Chicken, cooks them low and slow to bring out their pleasantly murky flavor. He seasons them with smoked turkey wings instead of bacon because some of his customers are watching their diets. A tip for Northerners: whatever you do, don't toss out the brothy remains of the pot, known as the potlikker. Instead, pour the hot liquid into a bowl, crumble in some cornbread, and give it a dash or two of pepper vinegar. According to some aficionados, that's the whole point of cooking collards.

Charles Gabriel's Long-Cooked Collards with Smoked Turkey

1 pound smoked turkey wings or
    drumstick

8 cups water

3 bunches (approximately 4 pounds)
    collards

8 tablespoons (1 stick) butter

1 medium onion, chopped

1 tablespoon salt

1 tablespoon freshly
    ground black pepper

2 tablespoons sugar

Put the turkey wings or drumstick in a large pot with 8 cups of water. Bring to a boil over high heat. Turn heat down and cook for 90 minutes. Meanwhile, clean the collards. Stem the leaves. Roll up a few leaves at a time, and cut them crosswise into ½-inch strips. Remove the turkey from the pot, pull the meat away from the bones, and carefully strain the stock of any errant bones. Discard the bones and tear the meat into small pieces, then stir it back into the pot. Add the butter, the chopped onion, and all the seasonings to the pot. Add the collards a few handfuls at a time, stirring them until all the greens are in the pot. Simmer over low heat for 1 hour. Remove collards from the pot with a slotted spoon. *Serves 4 to 6.*

BLACK SALSIFY

Salsify comes in two hues—the often gnarly white and the stick-like, bark-skinned black, a plant more accurately known as *scorzonera*. Both belong to the sunflower family and share a flavor that reminds some of oysters and others of artichokes. Even though Thomas Jefferson is said to have cultivated it, the root vegetable is more popular in Europe than it is here, where seasonally minded chefs like Damon Wise, late of Craft and now at Monkey Bar, are trying to raise its understated profile.

Damon Wise's Pan-Roasted Black Salsify

4 large salsify roots

Juice of 1 lemon

1 teaspoon black peppercorns

5 sprigs thyme

1 bay leaf

1 teaspoon coriander seeds

Kosher salt

1 to 2 tablespoons
   extra-virgin olive oil

Freshly ground black
   pepper to taste

1 tablespoon unsalted
   butter

Peel the salsify and place in a shallow pan with water to cover, lemon juice, peppercorns, 3 sprigs of thyme, bay leaf, coriander, and salt to taste. Bring to a simmer and cook until tender. Remove salsify from liquid and, once cooled, cut into batons of equal size. Heat sauté pan over medium heat and add olive oil. Add salsify and season with salt and pepper. Cook until golden brown. Add the butter and the remaining sprigs of thyme and toss until the butter foams. Remove from heat and transfer to paper towels. Serve immediately. ***Serves 4 to 6.***

BLOOD ORANGES

*I*s there another fruit besides the blood orange that elicits such a pleasurable response just by slicing into it? Although the color of its flesh varies from a striking deep red to a faint blush depending on the variety and where it was grown, the element of surprise is half the fun. The other half is its rich and vibrant citrus flavor—sweet-tart with a hint of berry that enhances everything from sauces to desserts. It pairs nicely with anchovy, garlic, and red onion, too, in this sharply seasoned winter salad from chef Jody Williams, who spent the bulk of her career cooking Italian before transitioning to French at Buvette.

Jody Williams's Insalata d'Arancia

1 anchovy fillet

½ teaspoon dried oregano

1 garlic clove, minced

2 tablespoons good red wine vinegar

Salt and freshly ground black pepper

½ cup extra-virgin olive oil

6 blood oranges

¼ cup julienned red onion, rinsed in cold water

4 basil leaves

¼ cup Kalamata olives, pitted

In a small bowl, beat anchovy, oregano, garlic, vinegar, and salt and pepper to taste. Slowly whisk in olive oil. Peel oranges, removing pith. Slice horizontally into thin rounds. Arrange in a single layer on a chilled serving plate. Garnish with onions, basil, and olives. Pour vinaigrette over salad and marinate 5 minutes. *Serves 4 to 6.*

GOOSE

Before opening such New York kitchens as Wallsé and Blaue Gans, chef Kurt Gutenbrunner grew up in Austria, where roast goose at Christmas is traditional. In recent years, he's begun serving the rich poultry as a holiday special but he also offers this recipe for any home cooks inspired to instigate a yuletide ritual of their own. For crisp skin and succulent meat, dry the bird in the fridge overnight, then prick the skin to release the fat, a prized commodity that can be repurposed for making crispy roast potatoes to accompany the main dish.

Kurt Gutenbrunner's Roast Christmas Goose

1 (10- to 12-pound) goose

3 onions, peeled (1 quartered, 2 cut into large dice)

3 carrots, cut into large dice

6 celery stalks, cut into large dice

Kosher salt

1 apple, quartered

1 orange, quartered

½ bunch fresh thyme

Salt and freshly ground black pepper

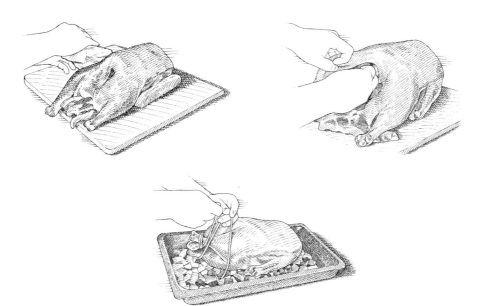

ONE DAY AHEAD: Remove giblets and reserve, covered, in the refrigerator. Using paper towels, dry the cavity and the exterior of the goose and place on a rack, uncovered, in the refrigerator overnight.

TO COOK: Remove goose from the refrigerator and bring to room temperature. Preheat oven to 350 degrees. If the bird is still moist, dry inside and out with paper towels. Scatter the diced onion, carrots, celery, and reserved giblets in the bottom of a large, shallow roasting pan. Generously salt the cavity and stuff with the quartered apple, orange, and onion, as well as the thyme. With a skewer or fork, prick the skin of the goose all over. Salt and pepper the outside of the bird, truss it, and place directly on top of the diced vegetables. Add 2 cups boiling water to the pan. Roast 2½ to 3 hours (drain some of the rendered fat from the pan periodically with a basting bulb, and reserve for roast potatoes), or until an instant-read thermometer reads 165 to 175 degrees and the juices run clear. If the skin is not crisp, increase the temperature to 375 degrees and cook for another 10 minutes. Allow the goose to rest for 30 minutes before carving. Serve with braised red cabbage and roasted potatoes. *Serves 6.*

CLEMENTINES

Citrus is winter's most revivifying bright spot, enlivening produce shelves and—if you're lucky enough to live in the right zone—local farmers' markets. At their best and sweetest, mandarins (a category that includes clementines and satsumas) are irresistible eaten out of hand. But they also work well in more elaborate compositions, like this plate of thinly sliced fruit served over a deep caramel flavored with citrus peel, a seasonal special at the Manhattan Basque restaurant Txikito. Chef-partner Alex Raij is a devotee of Kishu mandarins, a Superball-size Chinese variety she gets mail-ordered from Ojai, California. But clementines work just as well, their sweet-tart flavor balanced by a garnish of floral olive oil and crunchy sea salt.

Alex Raij's Clementine Carpaccio with Citrus Caramel, Sea Salt, and Olive Oil

12 seedless clementines (or 4 times as many Kishus), plus 4 to 6 more to yield 1 cup juice

Juice of 1 lemon

1 cup sugar

⅛ teaspoon salt

¼ cup Spanish olive oil (preferably Navarran Arbequina)

Crunchy sea salt

Peel 12 clementines by hand, reserving peel from 3. Chill fruit. Combine fruit juices and strain. Julienne the peels and place in a small pot, along with sugar. Cover with ⅔ cup water. Stir once and heat on medium-high flame. Boil until the caramel turns dark chestnut, then add citrus juices very carefully. Whisk the mixture and stir in salt. Let cool slightly or entirely at room temperature, but do not chill. To serve: Place 1½ tablespoons of the caramel on each of 4 plates. Using a very sharp knife and no pressure, thinly slice the peeled fruit crosswise into ⅛- to ¼-inch-thick wheels. Arrange in a petal pattern over the caramel without overlapping. Drizzle with olive oil and sprinkle a tiny amount of sea salt on each slice. *Serves 4.*

MAINE SHRIMP

The antithesis of the big bland jumbo variety, tiny sweet shrimp from Maine are usually available from late January through early March. These aristocrats of the crustacean world are so fine and fresh, you can gobble them down raw with just a drizzle of extra-virgin olive oil and a dash of sea salt. They're also pretty delicious wedged into a butter-toasted hot dog bun the way they do at Luke's Lobster in New York City. New Englanders will tell you that a shrimp roll is not a shrimp roll without a top-split wiener bun, but the more readily available side-split variety will do in a pinch.

Luke's Shrimp Roll

3 pounds fresh Maine shrimp

¼ teaspoon freshly ground black pepper

¼ teaspoon celery salt

¼ teaspoon garlic salt

¼ teaspoon dried thyme

¼ teaspoon oregano

8 tablespoons (1 stick)
   unsalted butter

4 hot dog buns

Juice of ¼ lemon

4 teaspoons mayonnaise

In a large pot, bring 2 quarts of salted water to a boil. Add the shrimp in batches and cook for 30 seconds. Twist off the heads and peel. Reserve peeled shrimp in refrigerator or over ice. (You can save the heads and shells to make a broth.) Mix the spices in a small bowl and reserve. Melt the butter in a small saucepan. Brush the insides of the buns with the melted butter, and toast over medium heat on grill pan or griddle until golden brown. Stir lemon juice into the remaining melted butter and reserve. Spread the insides of each toasted bun with 1 teaspoon of mayonnaise. Arrange equal amounts of shrimp in each bun. Drizzle the melted-butter-lemon mixture over the shrimp. Sprinkle with seasoning mixture to taste. *Serves 4.*

WINTER SPICES

*I*n self-styled "bar chef" Stefan Trummer's native Austria, vendors hawk hot wine on the sidewalk like pretzels. Until that happens in the United States, you'll have to replicate his cockles-warming recipe for winter sangria in the comfort of your own home. The aromatic mulled wine is fortified with cognac and rum, and the spices—cinnamon, star anise, allspice, and cloves—might remind you of Christmas, but their fragrant heat becomes crucial a month or two later, when winter really sets in.

Stefan Trummer's Winter Sangria

2 small slices pomegranate
  with peels

1 slice apple

1 slice pear

½ vanilla bean, scraped

1 large orange peel

6 ounces medium-bodied,
  fruity red wine

2 ounces dark rum

1 ounce cognac

2 ounces freshly squeezed
  orange juice

1 ounce honey

1 cinnamon stick

6 to 8 whole cloves

1 star anise

6 to 8 allspice berries

Combine ingredients in a saucepan. Cook over medium heat until the liquid starts to simmer. Then turn heat to high for about 10 seconds. Strain into a wine or punch glass, garnish with the fruit and the cinnamon stick, and serve with a spoon. ***Makes 1 drink***.

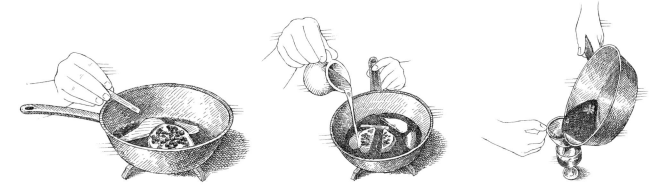

SQUID

A few things you may not know about squid: Along with their cephalopod cousins the octopus and the cuttlefish, they are the brainiacs of the mollusk family. Squid possess sacs that secrete ink (some believe in the shape of inky decoys) to flummox predators. They like to swim by the light of the moon, preferably backward, but become so transfixed by its allure, they have a tendency to beach themselves. (This isn't so smart, but it's certainly romantic.) As far as eating them goes, winter is when they're at their peak—or so says Esca's Dave Pasternack, who grills them, slices them, and tosses them into a parsley-radish salad.

Dave Pasternack's Grilled Calamari Salad

1 cup flat-leaf parsley, washed and dried

1 lemon

¼ teaspoon crushed red pepper flakes

1 teaspoon chopped fresh rosemary

1 pound fresh squid (tubes and heads),
    cleaned (remove beaks, eyes, innards,
    and ink sacs, or have your fishmonger
    do it for you)

¼ cup extra-virgin olive oil

5 radishes, washed

Salt and freshly ground black
    pepper to taste

Chile oil (optional)

Chop 2 tablespoons of parsley. Finely chop the zest of half a lemon. Place in mixing bowl with crushed pepper and rosemary. Add squid and toss with enough olive oil to coat. Marinate, covered, in the refrigerator overnight or at least 1 hour. Thinly slice radishes with mandoline. Place them in a large bowl and toss with remaining parsley leaves, juice from lemon, salt and pepper, and a splash of olive oil. Set aside. Over high heat, grill calamari on a cast-iron grill pan. Press down on the squid with a weight to mark; after approximately 3 minutes, flip and finish cooking for 2 to 3 minutes more. Remove from pan; toss squid in bowl with radishes and parsley to catch the cooking juices. Remove squid from bowl, slice into rings, and return to bowl. Divide into 4 portions and serve on plates garnished with a drizzle of chile oil or extra-virgin olive oil. *Serves 4.*

YUZU

Prized by chefs for its distinctive floral fragrance and complex lemon-lime flavor, the golf-ball–size *yuzu* is a fairly frost-resistant hybrid of an ancient citrus called *Ichang papeda* and a sour mandarin orange. Chef Josh DeChellis, formerly of New York's La Fonda del Sol, and an old *yuzu* pro from his days at Union Pacific, uses this quick marmalade recipe for everything from slathering on toast to spooning over ice cream.

Josh DeChellis's Ten-Minute Yuzu Marmalade

2 fresh yellow *yuzu*

½ cup sugar

½ cup unsalted *yuzu* juice, plus 1 teaspoon (available at Asian
   markets; you can also substitute unsalted *sudachi* juice or 1 ounce
   salted *yuzu* juice with 3 ounces lemon juice)

¼ cup elderflower syrup

4 tablespoons water

1 teaspoon pectin

Remove seeds from fresh *yuzu*, and chop the fruit roughly into approximately ½-inch pieces. Put chopped *yuzu* in a small saucepot. Add sugar, ½ cup of *yuzu* juice, elderflower syrup, and ¼ cup water. Cook over very low heat until the zest of the *yuzu* is soft (about 8 minutes). Taste and add more sugar if it is too bitter. Add the pectin and whisk until thickened. Remove from heat and cool. Add the remaining 1 teaspoon of *yuzu* juice. To serve: Add to salad dressings, meat sauces, or mix with wasabi paste and olive oil to dress a scallop seviche. ***Makes ½ cup.***

RADICCHIO DI CASTELFRANCO

*I*n the States, radicchio is a bit player in the salad kingdom, most commonly seen as the red component of the ubiquitous tricolore. In Italy, where varieties are named after towns of origin, the refreshingly bitter chicory is held in higher esteem, earning protected geographic status like cheese or wine. Typically available between November and March, the more obscure varieties, such as the speckled Castelfranco, the elongated Tardivo, and the endivelike Treviso, can be found in specialty shops that import them directly from the source. Together, they make a vibrant salad in this recipe from Salumeria Rosi's Cesare Casella.

Cesare Casella's Three-Radicchio Salad with Anchovy Dressing and Grana Padano

1 head radicchio di Castelfranco

1 head radicchio di Treviso

2 heads Tardivo

1 large garlic clove, or 2 small cloves

4 anchovy fillets, in salt, rinsed well

1 tablespoon fresh lemon juice

3 tablespoons extra-virgin olive oil

1 tablespoon red wine vinegar

1 tablespoon red wine

Salt and freshly ground black pepper to taste

4 ounces *grana padano*

Remove the leaves from the Castelfranco and cut into 4 pieces lengthwise. Remove the leaves from the Treviso and cut in half lengthwise. For the Tardivo, separate the leaves but keep whole. Place all leaves in a large bowl. Set aside. Using a mortar and pestle, mash the garlic and anchovy fillets until they reach a smooth, pastelike consistency. Whisking continuously, begin slowly adding the liquid ingredients until well combined. Add salt and pepper to taste. Continue to whisk. Add the dressing to the radicchio and gently toss to coat all the leaves. Taste for additional seasoning. Divide the salad onto four plates, and shave the *grana padano* on top. *Serves 4.*

*R*amps = spring.

Have you been to the Greenmarket in January? Trust me, nothing really grows in a New York winter—those damn apples were harvested in the summer. Without anything green or fresh coming from the market, it's shockingly easy for a chef to succumb to scurvy.

Sure, asparagus, morels, and fiddlehead ferns start popping up, but all after the ramp. Which is why I will always equate spring with ramps. The foraged wild onion native to the East Coast saturates New York City around late April to the end of May (depending on Mother Nature). And I would argue that outside of apples, there isn't anything that grows better in any season than the ramp.

Critics will argue that the ramp is overrated, overpriced, and overused in New York City. I might listen to them but they don't suffer the Sisyphean task of creating a menu in the despairs of winter. The season for ramps is so short that chefs never really get to enjoy them. I prefer the first ramps of the season, when they have a small bulb base, a tender stalk, and a zesty green leaf, because all you need to do is trim the stem and you are ready to go.

You can cook ramps every way possible, from pestos to pizzas. I prefer pickling them. Mix a batch of vinegar, water, sugar, and spices; boil and pour over cleaned ramps; and you're all set. Plan wisely and you will have a reminder of spring until the next batch of ramps sprouts.

—DAVID CHANG, CHEF/OWNER, MOMOFUKU

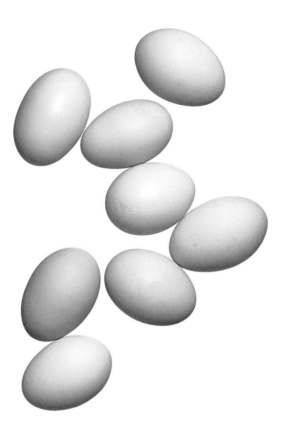

SPRING

ASPARAGUS

Before asparagus, the Goldilocks of springtime veggies, makes its celebrated annual appearance, the weather has to be just right—a little warm but not too. And no other vegetable loses its flavor and juiciness as rapidly after being picked as do these tender shoots. To enjoy them in all their fleeting glory, you needn't do more than boil them in salted water, sprinkle with salt and pepper, and serve with melted butter. For something a bit more exotic, do as Txikito's Alex Raij does: place the spears in a brown paper lunch bag and put the bag in the oven for a bit. When they're ready, remove the bag, shake the asparagus loose, and unleash the olfactory essence of spring throughout your kitchen.

Alex Raij's Asparagus en Bolsa

1 untreated small or medium brown
    paper lunch bag
Extra-virgin olive oil, as needed
1 bunch medium asparagus
Kosher salt to taste

Pinch of saffron
Juice of 1 lime
A knob of butter
8 medium shrimp, peeled, deveined,
    and chilled (optional)

Preheat oven to 450 degrees. Using a pastry brush, paint the inside of the paper bag with olive oil. (This waterproofs the bag and keeps it from scorching.) Holding asparagus spears closer to the bottom third, bend the stalk until it snaps, discarding the woody ends. (If the asparagus are too large for the bag, cut each spear in half on the bias.) Rinse under cold water, shake dry, and place in the bag. Season with salt, crumble in the saffron, and add the lime juice and butter. Season the optional shrimp with salt and add to the bag. Roll down the top of the bag and staple it shut. Place the bag on a baking sheet and bake until it's puffed out and sizzling, approximately 9 minutes. Remove sheet from oven and slide the bag onto a shallow platter. Holding bag from the top, give it a jerk or two until the bottom breaks and releases the asparagus and shrimp. *Serves 4.*

BURDOCK

*E*ven Euell Gibbons might have hesitated before tucking into a stick of burdock. In its raw state, the patchy root, aka *gobo* in Japan, seems better suited to a game of fetch than a toss in the sauté pan. Nevertheless, it has a deliciously earthy and subtly sweet flavor similar to an artichoke's, not to mention numerous purported health benefits. Scrub one down and try it in this recipe for *kinpira*, a traditional Japanese dish, from the *izakaya* Kasadela in New York's East Village.

Kasadela's Kinpira

1 medium burdock root, peeled

1 medium carrot, peeled

White wine vinegar

1½ tablespoons sesame oil

1 teaspoon sugar

1 tablespoon mirin (sweet rice wine)

2 tablespoons soy sauce

1 teaspoon white sesame seeds

Cut the burdock and carrot into matchstick-size pieces. Soak the julienned burdock in a bowl of water with a dash of vinegar for about 10 minutes, then drain and dry on paper towels. Put sesame oil in a medium pan over medium-high heat and sauté the burdock and carrot for about 5 minutes. Add sugar, mirin, soy sauce, and ¼ cup of water to pan. Reduce heat and cook until the liquid evaporates. Add the sesame seeds, mix, and serve. ***Serves 4 as an appetizer***.

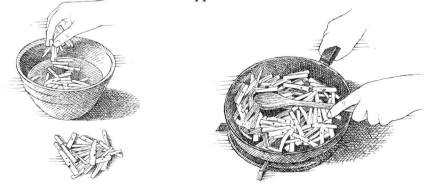

DUCK EGGS

Nothing against chickens, but according to a wizened egg expert we met roaming the Greenmarket one day, duck eggs have a greater ratio of yolk to whites, and are therefore "eggier." Casa Mono's opening chef Andy Nusser (now at Port Chester's Tarry Lodge) liked to serve them sunny-side up, drizzled with truffle vinaigrette, festooned with slivers of *mojama* (Spanish salt-cured tuna loin), and perched atop a Lincoln Log–like stack of fingerling potatoes. "Just a glorified fried egg," he says. Only eggier.

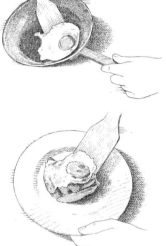

Andy Nusser's Fried Duck Eggs with Truffled Potatoes and Mojama

1 pound fingerling potatoes

Small jar (about 2 ounces) black truffle
    pieces or shavings

1 shallot, minced

2 tablespoons sherry vinegar

½ cup Spanish olive oil, plus additional
    for frying

Salt and freshly ground
    black pepper to taste

6 duck eggs

½ pound *mojama*

Boil fingerlings until tender. Strain, cool, and slice in half lengthwise. In a large bowl, combine truffles, shallot, sherry vinegar, and ½ cup olive oil. Brown potatoes in olive oil. Season with salt and pepper. Toss potatoes in the truffle vinaigrette. Fry eggs sunny-side up with olive oil in a nonstick pan. Plate the potatoes in a stack. Top with fried eggs, and add the sliced *mojama* over the top. ***Serves 6.***

FIDDLEHEAD FERNS

Think of fiddlehead ferns, those tightly coiled, emerald-green symbols of spring, as ferns interrupted. Left unforaged, they'd mature into tall, feathery fronds. Gathered young, they boast a crunchy texture and vegetal flavor prized by seasonally minded chefs. At the Spotted Pig, April Bloomfield sautés them with ramps and garlic for a particularly pungent, pancetta-enhanced bruschetta topping.

April Bloomfield's Fiddlehead Fern Bruschetta

10 ounces ramps

10 ounces fiddlehead ferns

4 tablespoons butter

Pinch of Maldon sea salt

Pinch of crushed red pepper flakes

2 garlic cloves (1 chopped, 1 halved)

Half a lemon

4 slices of rustic Italian bread

4 teaspoons olive oil

8 slices pancetta, cooked until crisp

Wash the ramps and the fiddlehead ferns well. Slice off and reserve the white bulbs of the ramps, and chop the green leaves into thirds. Melt the butter in a skillet over medium heat until it starts to froth. Add ferns, the ramp bulbs, sea salt, and red pepper flakes. Cook until vegetables are slightly soft, approximately 2 minutes. Add the ramp leaves. Toss and check seasoning. Cook until slightly brown (approximately 3 minutes). Add the chopped garlic. Turn off heat. Drizzle lightly with lemon. Toast or grill the bread until brown. Rub lightly with halved garlic clove and drizzle with olive oil. Top with ferns, ramps, and pancetta. *Serves 4.*

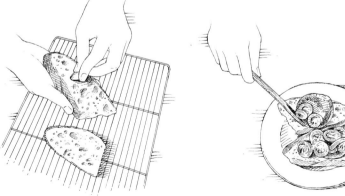

MAPLE SYRUP

March is high season for New York and Vermont sugar-makers, who tap maples for the sap that they boil down into syrup. The new crop of "fancy," the lightest grade, usually shows up first at farmers' markets, followed by grade A medium and dark amber, and then finally deepest, darkest grade B. The last's pure expression of maple flavor is the secret ingredient behind Charles Kiely and Sharon Pachter's "Grocery bars." The owners of Brooklyn's highly acclaimed Grocery restaurant bake these tasty treats twice a week for the staff to snack on, which must help them earn those stratospheric Zagat scores.

Charles Kiely and Sharon Pachter's Grocery Bars

3 cups rolled oats

½ cup wheat germ

¼ cup flour

1 cup walnuts, chopped

12 dates, chopped

1 cup grade B maple syrup

3 eggs

1 cup applesauce

½ cup peanut butter

Preheat oven to 350. Combine the dry ingredients. Combine the wet ingredients. Add wet to dry and mix well. Press into a parchment-lined sheet tray, about 1 inch thick. Bake until a toothpick comes out clean, approximately 30 minutes.

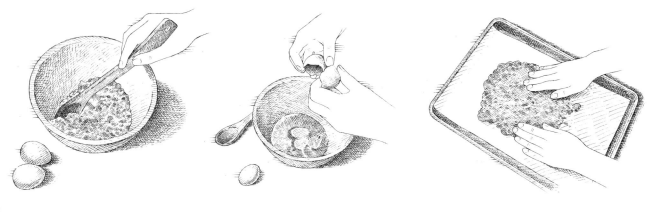

GREEN ALMONDS

S o-called green almonds are harvested in that brief window before their shells have hardened and the nuts have fully formed. Mediterranean and Middle Eastern cultures have long enjoyed them in their fuzzy green state, with their grassy, vegetal flavor and unripe crunch, while in America they remain a relative rarity. Public chef Brad Farmerie is a devoted fan of the spring delicacy's natural acidity and raw texture, which he highlights in this exceedingly simple riff on the Southeast Asian street snack green mango with chile salt.

Brad Farmerie's
Green Almonds with Chile Salt

2 tablespoons sugar

2½ teaspoons salt

1 teaspoon *shichimi togarashi* (Japanese chile mix)

3 tablespoons light olive oil

1 dozen green almonds, washed

Combine the sugar, salt, and *shichimi togarashi* in a small serving vessel and mix well. Place the oil in a separate bowl. Dip the green almonds first in the oil, then in the chile-salt mix. ***Serves 2***.

GREEN GARLIC

Fetishized ramps tend to steal the springtime spotlight, but don't make the mistake of overlooking green garlic (aka spring garlic, young garlic, and baby garlic)—splendidly odoriferous in its own right, with a comparatively mellow flavor. The allium makes its annual appearance just in time for cookout season, presenting the perfect opportunity to sample it in Gramercy Tavern chef Michael Anthony's recipe for a pungent and delicious steak sauce.

Michael Anthony's Green Garlic Sauce

2 bunches green garlic

1 teaspoon olive oil

1 teaspoon *colatura* (cured anchovy sauce, available at Italian specialty stores)

1 cup beef or chicken stock

Trim away most of the leafy greens from the green garlic, saving about an inch of the lower green. Cut off the root end of each shoot, then clean, dry, and finely chop garlic. In a pan, sauté the garlic in the olive oil over medium heat until tender. Deglaze with the *colatura*, and add the beef or chicken stock. Simmer for 1 minute. Spoon generously over grilled flatiron (top blade) or flank steak, and serve atop a bed of chopped and sautéed spring onions. **Serves 4**.

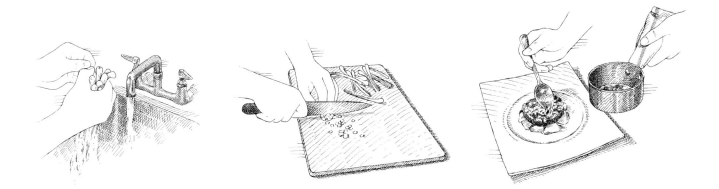

NEW-CATCH HOLLAND HERRING

For Manhattan herring lovers, June is the busiest month. That's when the restaurant Aquavit holds its annual Herring Week and when the Hollandse Nieuwe (or New-Catch Holland herring) arrives at Russ & Daughters, New York's venerable and preeminent appetizing store. Unlike the excellent firm-fleshed and variously pickled herring sold at the shop year-round, these mouth-waterers are soft and buttery and just barely cured on deck as soon as they're caught.

The best way to eat a New-Catch Holland herring is as soon as possible—at the point of purchase, even. If you're so inclined, no one will stop you from doing so at the Russ & Daughters counter. There is a technique, however. According to co-owner Joshua Russ Tupper, the way to do it is to chop up some white onion, grab the herring fillets by the tail, and roll them around in the onion. Tilt your head back, and basically lower the fish into your mouth like a Hanna-Barbera cartoon cat. *Serves 1.*

GOAT'S-MILK CHEESE

With kidding season over in early April, it's all systems go for goat-cheese-making at the country's burgeoning farmstead dairies, and *fromage* made from the first milk of the year starts showing up at nearby farmers' markets and local cheesemongers. Find a creamy, velvety wheel like this ash-streaked specimen from Vermont's Blue Ledge Farm and combine it with ramps in a grilled cheese sandwich for a delectably pungent springtime snack.

Grilled Goat Cheese and Ramp Sandwiches

12 ramps

Salt and freshly ground black pepper
    to taste

2 tablespoons extra-virgin olive oil

8 slices of rustic sandwich bread

12 ounces goat cheese, crumbled and
    rind removed

4 tablespoons butter, softened

Preheat oven to broil. Wash and dry the ramps. Trim the roots and cut the ramps into approximately 1½-inch pieces. Place the ramps in a bowl, season with salt and pepper, and toss with the olive oil. Place the ramps on a baking sheet and cook until they are slightly charred, about 3 minutes. Lay out 4 slices of the bread and spread each evenly with equal amounts of cheese. Top each slice with the ramps. Cover with the remaining slices of bread. Generously butter the outsides of each sandwich. Over medium-low heat in a large cast-iron skillet or on a griddle, cook each side of the sandwiches until golden brown, using another pan or a full teakettle to weight them down. ***Serves 4.***

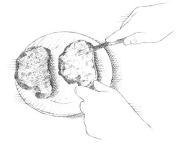 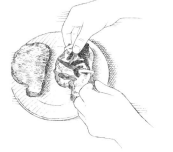 

MÂCHE

Although you'd never know by its dainty appearance, mâche is a hardy thing, capable of being sown in the fall for a late-winter or spring harvest. That makes the velvety lettuce with the fancy French name (aka lamb's tongue or corn salad) a good interim green, its graceful rosettes proffering a burst of delicately sweet, mildly nutty flavor when we need it most. Chef Akhtar Nawab contrasted its soft texture with the crunch of watermelon radish in a brisk early-spring salad when he was chef at Manhattan's Craftbar, mere blocks from the Union Square Greenmarket.

Akhtar Nawab's Mâche
and Watermelon-Radish Salad

1 pound mâche

1 small watermelon radish

2 tablespoons Dijon mustard

1 tablespoon acacia honey

1 tablespoon red wine vinegar

1 tablespoon sherry vinegar

2 medium shallots, finely minced

⅛ cup extra-virgin olive oil

Salt and freshly ground black pepper
to taste

Trim the ends of the mâche leaves. Rinse and dry. Peel the radish with a vegetable peeler and slice thinly with a mandoline. In a medium bowl, add mustard, honey, vinegars, and half of the minced shallots. Whisk until combined. Slowly drizzle in olive oil, continuing to whisk until emulsified, and season with salt and pepper. In a large bowl, combine the mâche, the remaining minced shallots, the sliced radish, and the vinaigrette until the leaves are well coated. Adjust seasoning and serve immediately. *Serves 4 to 6.*

LEEKS

In Spain, springtime is welcomed with a *calçotada*, the annual flame-licked ritual of grilling *calçots*, a sort of sweet, tender spring onion, over an open fire. Peter Hoffman imported the custom to Soho, where he hosted his version of the seasonal celebration at Savoy, the pioneering locavore restaurant he's since transformed into the more casual Back Forty West. For his version, Hoffman substitutes locally grown overwintered leeks (plants that have survived in the ground all winter to be harvested early in spring), and serves them, in authentic Catalonian fashion, with pungent *romesco* sauce as the messy finger-food kickoff of a three-course feast. It's a tradition worth incorporating into your own backyard grill repertoire—chilled rosé and plenty of wet naps strongly recommended.

Peter Hoffman's Grilled Leeks with Romesco

¼ cup olive oil, plus more for frying

2 small slices sourdough bread

3 garlic cloves, roughly chopped

½ cup almonds, toasted

2 large dried ancho chiles, soaked overnight and seeded

1½ cups canned plum tomatoes, liquid reserved

1 tablespoon *pimentón*

¼ cup red wine vinegar

Juice of ½ lemon

Salt

2 or 3 bunches leeks

FOR *ROMESCO*: Heat half an inch of olive oil in a sauté pan and fry bread, browning both sides. In a food processor, grind bread, garlic, and almonds. Process until fine. Add the anchos, tomatoes, and *pimentón*. Purée until smooth. Add the olive oil, vinegar, and lemon juice, and purée. If texture isn't loose enough to work as a dip, add either water, reserved tomato juice, or more lemon juice, depending on taste. Season with salt.

FOR LEEKS: Clean leeks well by making 2 slits in the stalk, from just below where it turns green up toward the leaves, and rinse thoroughly under cold running water. Rub them with a bit of olive oil. Grill outdoors over fairly high heat until they char and blacken considerably (2 to 3 minutes per side; thicker leeks will take longer). Pile leeks in a heap, and let rest 5 minutes to allow heat to penetrate. When they've cooled, peel back the charred outer layer and dip the soft hearts in the *romesco* sauce. ***Serves 6 to 8.***

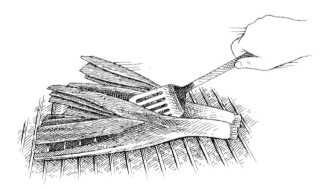

LOVAGE

Think of lovage as celery gone wild, or at least as celery that has successfully completed an assertiveness training course. The perennial herb has a celerylike fragrance and flavor so intense, it's been used in soaps and deodorants, not to mention love potions. It's also good in soups and salads, and, especially, in this newfangled gravlax recipe from *Chopped* judge Amanda Freitag, who served the dish when she cooked at the Harrison in Manhattan's Tribeca.

Amanda Freitag's Lovage Gravlax with Potato and Herb Salad

FOR THE GRAVLAX

1 cup kosher salt

¾ cup sugar

2 tablespoons coriander seed, cracked

1½ pounds arctic char fillet (ask your
    fishmonger to fillet a side of the fish)

1 bunch lovage leaves, chopped

2 lemons (1 sliced, 1 juiced)

FOR THE POTATO-HERB SALAD

½ pound new potatoes

¼ cup lovage leaves

¼ cup Italian parsley leaves

½ cup frisée, cleaned and roughly chopped

½ cup lemon juice

½ cup extra-virgin olive oil

Salt and freshly ground black pepper

FOR THE GRAVLAX: In a small mixing bowl, blend together the salt, sugar, and coriander. Sprinkle about a quarter of the spice mixture lengthwise down the center of a sheet of plastic wrap long enough to fit the fish, then place fillet skin side down on top of the spice mix. Sprinkle remaining gravlax spice on top of the fillet, pressing it into the fillet to thoroughly coat. Sprinkle lovage on top of the spice. Place sliced lemons on the fillet, and pour lemon juice over the top. Wrap fillet tightly in plastic wrap, place on a baking sheet or baking dish, and refrigerate for at least 24 hours. Remove from refrigerator and carefully remove plastic wrap. With a paper towel, gently wipe off all the remaining spice. With a 12-inch slicing knife, slice fish very thin horizontally and place the shingled slices between two pieces of parchment paper. Wrap in plastic and refrigerate.

FOR THE POTATO-HERB SALAD: In a medium pot, boil unpeeled potatoes in salted water until tender; remove from water and place in a bowl to let cool. Once cool, slice potatoes thinly, about the size of silver dollars. In a medium mixing bowl, toss them with lovage, parsley, frisée, lemon juice, and extra-virgin olive oil. Season with salt and pepper to taste. Serve alongside the gravlax. *Serves 6.*

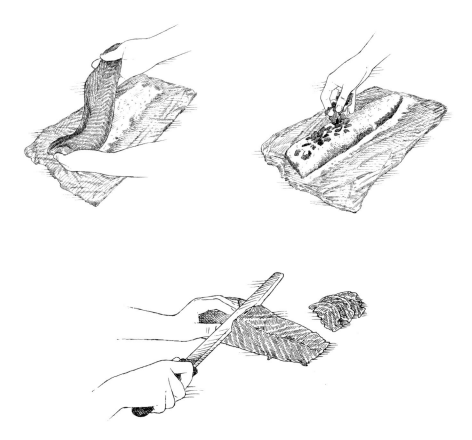

MANGOES

Tropical fruit like mango is a sweet, tangy bridge between winter's citrus and the first good berries of spring. Look for virtually fiberless varieties, like creamy Mexican Ataulfos and India's renowned Alphonsos, which make for smooth-as-silk *lassi*s in this recipe from Park Avenue restaurant pastry chef Richard Leach.

Richard Leach's Mango Lassi

1 ripe mango (approximately ¾ cup, cubed)

2 cups goat's-milk yogurt

½ cup sugar, or to taste (the sweeter the fruit, the less you'll need)

Slice mango lengthwise along the seed. Score the fruit both lengthwise and widthwise, then invert so cubes protrude from skin. Slice them off, and repeat procedure with the other half of the fruit, then slice, skin, and dice the remaining fruit around the seed. Combine with yogurt and sugar in a blender and purée at medium speed until smooth. If necessary, pass through a fine strainer and serve. *Serves 2.*

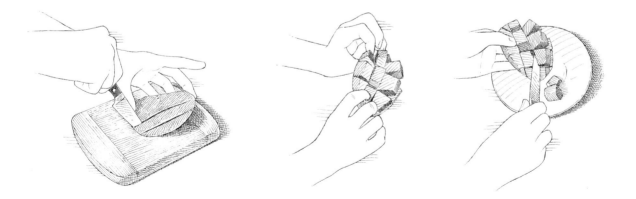

MORELS

Fresh wild honeycombed morels make their otherworldly appearance in April and usually stick around until early July. Like that of their truffle cousins, their flavor is deep, smoky, earthy, and a bit mysterious. Bertrand Chemel, the chef of 2941 Restaurant in Falls Church, Virginia, and formerly of New York's Café Boulud, recommends washing them carefully (to remove any sand) and cooking them simply with herbs and cream to enhance but not mask their supreme mushroominess. Serve them as a side dish with beef, lamb, or poultry, or, for a double dose of springtime delight, spoon over blanched asparagus.

Bertrand Chemel's Morel Fricassée

20 ounces fresh morels

2 teaspoons white wine vinegar

1 sprig thyme

2 bay leaves, dry or fresh

3 fresh sage leaves

3 sprigs tarragon

3 tablespoons unsalted butter

2 shallots, finely chopped

Salt and freshly ground black pepper

⅓ cup dry vermouth

½ cup heavy cream

5 sprigs chervil

Trim morel stems at bottom of caps and discard stems. Rinse the caps in up to five changes of cold water combined with the white vinegar. Shake morels well in the water, then pat dry on a towel. With butcher string, tie together the sprig of thyme, the bay and sage leaves, and one of the sprigs of tarragon to make a small herb bouquet. In a large, deep sauté pan over low heat, melt the butter. Add shallots to pan with herb bouquet and cook, stirring, approximately 2 minutes. Add morels, and salt and pepper to taste. Cover and continue to cook over medium heat another 2 minutes or so. Add the vermouth and stir well to deglaze. Cover and continue cooking approximately 3 minutes. Add the cream and cook uncovered, stirring occasionally, for about 5 minutes. Adjust seasoning and remove the herb bouquet. Stem remaining tarragon sprigs and the chervil, and sprinkle leaves over the morels. *Serves 4.*

PEA SHOOTS

The amazing thing about pea shoots is how faithfully they mimic the fresh, vegetal flavor of the pea itself. They're like the experimental three-course-dinner gum Violet Beauregarde chomps on despite Willy Wonka's admonishments, but with all the kinks worked out. Sautéing a few handfuls with pine nuts and raisins, as in the recipe that Salt Lake City chef Ryan Lowder developed when he ran the kitchen at New York's Mercat, only enhances their sweetness—which is a good thing for those who can't wait until the peas themselves arrive later in the season.

Ryan Lowder's Catalan Pea Shoots

1 pound (roughly 4 large handfuls) pea shoots

½ cup pine nuts

½ cup raisins

2 tablespoons unsalted butter

Salt

2 tablespoons extra-virgin olive oil

Wash and stem the pea shoots. Over medium-high heat, in a pan large enough to hold the shoots, cook the pine nuts and raisins in the butter until the nuts start to brown. Add shoots and a pinch of salt, stir, and turn constantly until shoots cook down and are incorporated with the other ingredients (this should take 30 seconds to 1 minute). Check seasoning and add salt if necessary. Leave excess butter in the pan, and finish with a drizzle of olive oil. *Serves 4.*

PHEASANT EGGS

As far as specialty eggs go, the khaki-colored pheasant variety is vastly underrated: It has a high yolk-to-white ratio and a rich flavor, but compared with a chicken egg, a lower level of cholesterol. Plus, when gently poached, it fits neatly atop a slice of toasted baguette, the centerpiece of this überseasonal salad. It was created by inveterate farmers' marketer Patti Jackson when she ran the kitchens of Centovini and I Trulli in Manhattan, but with its bounty of ingredients procured from the Union Square Greenmarket (asparagus, rhubarb, eggs, and miner's lettuce, aka claytonia), it might be more accurate to say she foraged it.

Patti Jackson's Miner's Lettuce Salad with Roasted Asparagus, Rhubarb, Pancetta, and Poached Pheasant Egg

1 tablespoon lemon juice

4 tablespoons extra-virgin olive oil, plus a little more for asparagus and bread

1 teaspoon finely diced chives

2 bunches miner's lettuce

1 stalk rhubarb, trimmed and cut in very fine dice

½ cup rice wine vinegar

½ teaspoon sugar

1 bunch small asparagus

Salt and freshly ground black pepper to taste

4 very thin slices pancetta

4 thin slices white country baguette

1 teaspoon distilled white vinegar

4 pheasant eggs

Preheat oven to 400 degrees. To make dressing, blend together lemon juice, olive oil, and chives; set aside. Pick through miner's lettuce, removing excess stems and weedy bits. Place rhubarb in a small container. In a small pan, scald rice wine vinegar with sugar, and pour over rhubarb; set aside to cool. Trim asparagus to 3-inch spears; reserve stems for another use. Toss asparagus with a little olive oil, salt, and pepper, and place on a baking dish. Lay out pancetta slices on another baking dish. Put asparagus in oven for 3 to 4 minutes, until just cooked. Bake pancetta in the same oven until crispy, 8 to 9 minutes; drain on paper towels. Brush bread slices with olive oil, and toast. Bring 2 quarts of water with a pinch of salt and 1 teaspoon white vinegar to a simmer. Carefully break the pheasant eggs; their shells can be very thick. Poach the eggs for 2 to 3 minutes. Remove eggs with a slotted spoon, and place on toast slices. Toss asparagus, drained rhubarb, and miner's lettuce with dressing. Season with salt and pepper. Place salad on 4 plates and top each with a pancetta slice and an egg on toast. Sprinkle with salt and pepper. *Serves 4.*

PINEAPPLE

A third of the world's pineapples come from Hawaii, and although they're available year-round, aficionados say they're at their best from spring to early summer. You don't need us to tell you that to fully enjoy a pineapple all that's necessary is to find a ripe one (they don't sweeten once they're picked) and slice away its peel. The supremely juicy, sweet-tart flesh needs no embellishment. If you really want to expand your pineapple horizons, though, we submit the following Australian-inspired recipe courtesy of Brooklyn's Five Leaves restaurant. It will doubtless exasperate purists of both the subtropical fruit and hamburger persuasions, but it's bound to win over a few skeptics.

Five Leaves (Pineapple) Burger

1 pineapple

2 cups rice wine vinegar

2 tablespoons honey

1 teaspoon whole coriander seeds

1 teaspoon whole black peppercorns

1 tablespoon mustard seed oil

1 ounce fresh ginger, peeled and
    thinly sliced

2 pounds grass-fed ground beef

Salt and freshly ground black pepper

1 tablespoon *harissa*

4 tablespoons mayonnaise

Juice and zest of 1 lime

4 eggs

4 hamburger buns, buttered and grilled

4 slices pickled beets

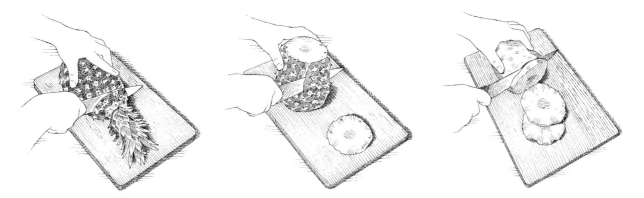

FOR THE PINEAPPLE: To peel, place pineapple on its side and, using a chef's knife, cut off a slice near the crown and another near the base. Stand pineapple on one of its ends and cut off a slice of skin a section at a time. With a tiny fruit baller or the tip of a potato peeler, remove the eyes. Slice 4 rounds approximately ½ inch thick and trim out the core from each slice. Save remaining pineapple for another use. Set rings in a nonreactive container. Place the rice wine vinegar, honey, coriander, peppercorns, mustard seed oil, and ginger in a pot and boil for about 5 minutes. Pour mixture over pineapple and refrigerate overnight.

FOR THE BURGERS: Divide beef into 4 patties. Season with salt and pepper. Grill to preferred temperature. Meanwhile, in a small bowl, mix the *harissa* with mayonnaise, lime juice, and zest; reserve. Grill pineapple rings (on a section of the grill or grill pan that's been lightly brushed with oil). In a skillet, cook the eggs sunny side up.

TO SERVE: Spread each side of the buns with the *harissa* mayo. Place the burgers on the buns and layer with grilled pineapple, pickled beets, and an egg. *Serves 4.*

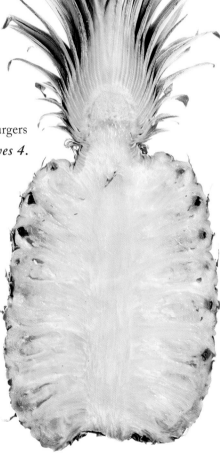

RAMPS

On the East Coast, where ramps grow wild, they are the first plantlike sign of early spring life, and thus seized upon by winter-weary chefs and locavore cooks with the kind of fervor usually associated with iPhone unveilings. Not bad for a broad-leaved allium malodorous enough to make the milder-mannered scallion or leek blush. Eating raw ramps can be done but it's not for the meek. When cooked, their characteristic sharpness mellows into a weirdly delicious funkiness. They're terrific in just about any recipe that calls for green garlic or spring onions. Traditionalists, however, cook their ramps with bacon and eggs. The only way to improve upon that dish is to add more ramps to it—preferably ones that have been quick-pickled in the manner of Momofuku's David Chang.

David Chang's Pickled Ramps

4 cups water

2 cups rice wine vinegar

2 cups sugar

2 tablespoons kosher salt

1 heaping teaspoon *shichimi togarashi* (Japanese spice mix)

1 pound ramps

In a medium saucepan, bring the water, vinegar, sugar, salt, and *shichimi togarashi* to a full boil, until sugar dissolves. Young ramps with small leaves may be pickled whole. Later in the season, as they grow larger, trim the top of the ramp leaf, leaving about 1 inch of green. (Save tops for other uses, like stock or pasta.) To clean ramps, use a paring knife to trim the root base. Peel the outer layer of skin and wash ramps well. Place cleaned ramps into a pickling container (lidded plastic is fine) and pour boiling liquid over them. Weigh down with a heavy bowl so that ramps are completely submerged. Let cool to room temperature, and store covered in refrigerator for up to a week. Serve with roasted ramps and bacon and eggs.

*I*t's helpful, during their brief season, to have several ramp recipes on hand. After all, a bunch festering in your crisper drawer is not a pretty thing. So once you've pickled, and roasted, and sautéed, try stirring some into this lush risotto from Scarpetta chef Scott Conant.

Scott Conant's Ramp Risotto

5 tablespoons extra-virgin
    olive oil

4 ramps

1 small shallot, finely chopped

Pinch of dried red pepper flakes

1 cup Vialone nano rice

½ cup dry white wine

4 cups chicken broth,
    simmering in a separate
    pot on stove

1 tablespoon unsalted butter

2 tablespoons grated
    Parmigiano-Reggiano cheese

Kosher salt to taste

In a wide, heavy-bottomed saucepan, heat 3 tablespoons olive oil over medium-high heat. Finely chop ramp greens and stalks, reserving greens for later. Add shallot, ramp stalks, and pepper flakes to the saucepan and stir until the shallot is translucent, about 2 minutes. Add rice and cook over medium heat for 2 minutes, stirring to coat rice with oil. Pour in ¼ cup of the wine and boil until almost absorbed; a little liquid should remain on top of the rice. Add ¼ to ½ cup of hot broth at a time, stirring the rice constantly until almost all of the liquid is absorbed. Add another ¼ cup of stock, the remaining wine, and a tablespoon of olive oil, continuing to stir. Add the ramp greens and more stock as needed and continue cooking and stirring until the risotto looks creamy but is still al dente, about 18 to 22 minutes. Remove from heat and let the risotto stand for about 30 seconds. Add a drizzle of olive oil, the butter, and the grated cheese; stir until well combined. Season with salt. ***Serves 4 as an appetizer.***

RHUBARB

Rhubarb is the locavore pastry chef's ramp: a springy sign of life when even the most devoted farmers' market shopper is beginning to think that if he never sees another storage apple, it will be too soon. Sweeten it with sugar, and you have the makings of a first-rate filling for a pie, tart, or galette. Or if you have summer on the brain, do as the people behind artisanal upstart People's Pops do, make creamy, refreshing ice pops.

People's Pops' Rhubarb Ice Pops

1 pound rhubarb

½ cup water, plus more to cover
    rhubarb

½ cup sugar

1 cinnamon stick

¼ cup plus 1 tablespoon
    heavy cream

FOR THE RHUBARB: Wash and chop the rhubarb into 1-inch pieces. Place rhubarb in wide-bottomed, nonreactive pot, and add approximately 1 inch of water, or enough to cover the rhubarb. Cover the pot, and cook over medium heat until the rhubarb breaks down into a lumpy purée, about 15 to 20 minutes. Strain the purée from its juice and reserve both.

FOR THE SIMPLE SYRUP: In a small pot, combine ½ cup of water with the sugar. Add the cinnamon stick. Gently heat the mixture, stirring occasionally, until the sugar is dissolved. Remove from the burner, discard the cinnamon stick, and let the syrup cool.

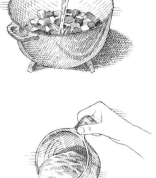

FOR THE ICE POPS: In a pitcher, combine the rhubarb purée and the simple syrup. Adjust sweetness—keeping in mind that some sweetness will dissipate upon freezing—by adding some of the reserved rhubarb juice. (Save remaining juice for another use.) Blend in cream. Pour mixture into ten 3-ounce ice-pop molds and freeze overnight. *Makes 10 ice pops.*

SHEEP'S-MILK RICOTTA

Seasonal eaters with a decidedly dairy-loving bent insist that spring hasn't officially sprung until the lambing season ends and the fresh sheep's-milk ricotta arrives. The luscious, creamy substance, made from the whey by-product of cheesemaking, is terrific on its own or with a drizzle of honey, but equally spectacular for making gnocchi, cavatelli, cheesecake, even *panna cotta*.

Sara Jenkins's Sheep's-Milk Ricotta Panna Cotta

1½ cups heavy cream

1¼ teaspoons unflavored gelatin

¼ cup sugar

Finely grated zest of 1 orange

Half a vanilla bean, split

½ cup sheep's-milk ricotta

3 large egg whites

6 teaspoons pistachio oil

6 teaspoons pistachios, toasted and chopped

Combine ¼ cup of the cream with gelatin in a bowl and let gelatin soften. Combine remaining cream, sugar, orange zest, and vanilla bean in a saucepan, bring to a low boil, and boil for 3 minutes. Remove from heat and remove the vanilla bean. Scrape seeds from bean and add to cream. Strain hot cream through a fine-mesh strainer into bowl with gelatin mixture; discard orange zest. Rice and whisk the ricotta into the cream. Whisk until gelatin is totally dissolved. Set bowl over an ice bath and stir until cooled to room temperature. Stiffly beat the egg whites and gently whisk half of the whites into the ricotta mixture, then fold in the other half. Transfer mixture to 4 individual dessert cups and let set in refrigerator, covered, for at least 3 hours. Garnish with a drizzle of pistachio oil and sprinkled toasted pistachios. *Serves 4.*

SCALLIONS

On the allium-appreciation scale, workaday scallions take a backseat to the seasonally anticipated spring onion and green garlic. (To complicate matters, the term *scallion* also applies to a growing stage in the life of the onion, the leek, the shallot, and the true scallion itself.) But despite the plant's supermarket ubiquity, cooks shouldn't underestimate its versatility. What would our soups, salads, and sesame noodles be without them? To say nothing of the iconic scallion pancake, explicated here by Danji chef Hooni Kim. His secret? Club soda and a frosty batter.

Hooni Kim's Pajeon

FOR THE PANCAKES

1 cup flour

¼ cup cornstarch

1 teaspoon baking powder

1 cup club soda

1 teaspoon grated garlic

1 tablespoon soy sauce

1 teaspoon sugar

FOR THE DIPPING SAUCE

2 tablespoons soy sauce

1 teaspoon rice vinegar

1 teaspoon mirin

3 drops sesame oil

1 egg yolk

A pinch of salt and freshly ground black
  pepper

1 bunch scallions

3 tablespoons vegetable oil, plus more
  as needed

FOR THE PANCAKES: In a bowl, mix all the ingredients for the batter and let cool in the refrigerator or freezer until very cold. (The colder the batter, the crisper the pancake.) Trim the ends off the scallions and cut into 1-inch pieces. If the white ends are thick, split them lengthwise before cutting them into pieces. Add the scallions to the cold batter. In a medium sauté pan over high heat, heat the vegetable oil until very hot. Using a 2-ounce ladle, add the batter to the pan, cooking 1 pancake at a time, and reduce heat to medium. Cook until bottom is golden brown and crisp. Flip pancake, and sauté until cooked through. Remove to paper toweling to absorb some of the grease. Repeat with remaining batter, adding more oil as needed. Cut pancakes into quarters and serve with the dipping sauce.

FOR THE SAUCE: In a small bowl, mix all the dipping sauce ingredients.

SOFT-SHELL CRABS

Not a separate species, as some landlubbers think, soft-shell crabs from Chesapeake Bay are blue crabs that have temporarily dropped their guard and shed their armor, allowing easier access to their tasty flesh. As in stand-up comedy, timing and delivery are everything in the soft-shell crab game: within twenty-four hours of shedding, a new shell emerges and the crabs are back in business. The trick is catching them right before they molt. No easy task. Simply dredged in cornmeal and pan-fried in butter, soft-shells are hard to beat. There is some slightly nasty work involved in cleaning them, but your neighborhood fishmonger can take care of that. Their distinctive crisp-and-tender texture also plays well against a squishy-soft Chinese steamed bun, as in this recipe that ran at David Chang's original Momofuku Noodle Bar.

Momofuku Noodle Bar's Soft-Shell Crab Buns

1 small-to-medium Kirby cucumber

½ teaspoon coarse salt and ½ teaspoon
    sugar mixed together

4 slices bacon

3 jumbo soft-shell crabs, cleaned

Salt and freshly ground black pepper to taste

6 Chinese steamed buns
    (available at Asian groceries)

Hoisin sauce

1 scallion, thinly sliced

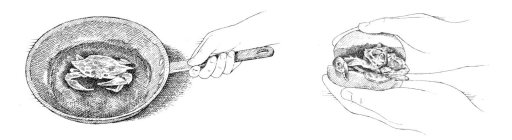

Thinly slice cucumber. In shallow bowl, mix cucumber slices with the salt and sugar until lightly coated. Let stand for about 2 hours to sweat them, then drain off liquid.

Heat a large sauté pan over high heat. Add bacon and render a couple of tablespoons of fat. Remove bacon and reserve for another use. Season crabs with salt and pepper and place them upside down in the pan, cooking each side for about 3 minutes. Meanwhile, steam 6 buns according to the package's instructions. Remove crabs from pan and slice each one in half. Spread about a tablespoon of hoisin sauce on the inside of each bun. Layer one side of bun with a few cucumber slices. Place a half crab on top of cucumbers and sprinkle with scallions. Fold the bun in half like a taco.

Makes 6 crab buns.

SORREL

Sorrel, the arrowhead-shaped herb and member of the buckwheat family that's prized for its inherently tart, lemony flavor, is traditionally used in cream soups and fish sauces. At Prune, Gabrielle Hamilton adds diced potatoes to her smooth sorrel purée but leaves them chunky for added texture. What the chef is aiming for is a bright and tangy potage with a soft, creamy foundation—a vibrantly sour, deeply rich dose of spring.

Gabrielle Hamilton's Sorrel Soup

Kosher salt

1 large russet potato, peeled and
    cut in ½-inch dice, reserved in cold
    water

8 tablespoons (1 stick) unsalted butter

1 large shallot, finely diced

1 pound sorrel, washed well

4 cups chicken stock

1 cup heavy cream

Freshly ground black pepper

Add 2 teaspoons kosher salt to 1 cup of water in a small saucepan and bring to a boil over high heat. Add potato and cook until water begins to return to a boil (pieces should be neither crunchy nor mushy and should hold their shape). Drain and reserve water. Melt 3 tablespoons butter in a soup pot over medium-low heat and sweat shallots until translucent. Chop sorrel and add to shallots. Cook briefly, until sorrel changes color from bright to drab green. Add chicken stock, potato cooking water, and salt and pepper to taste. Bring to boil and shut off. Carefully blend in batches while hot, adding a chunk of butter to each batch, until silky smooth. Return blended soup to pot, add cream, and adjust seasoning. To serve, distribute potatoes among 6 soup bowls and pour liquid over them. *Serves 6.*

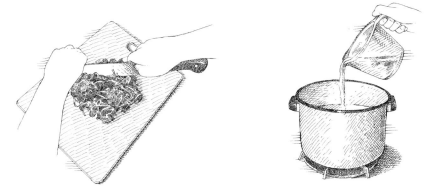

SPINACH

*U*ntil the weather gets hot, it's a good time for spinach, a plant that's often cooked into oblivion—a form of vegetable abuse that's all too easy to perpetrate on the insta-wilting, delicate leaves. With the right light touch, though, spinach surprises—even as a cold side dish like Japanese *oshitashi*. In the spirit of that sushi-bar staple, Del Posto's Mark Ladner makes a hot-and-cold spinach that gets its heat from chile peppers and its refreshing cool from a stint in the deep freeze. Dress it with a smooth Italian lemon oil or, in a nod to *oshitashi*'s bonito flakes, garnish it with *bottarga*.

Mark Ladner's Hot and Cold Spinach

2 bunches fresh young spinach

1½ tablespoons crushed red pepper flakes

¾ cup extra-virgin olive oil

Large pinch sea salt flakes

1 fresh medium finger chile, chopped

Zest of 1 lemon, chopped

½ cup lemon Agrumato oil

Remove roots from spinach. Soak the leaves, then rinse and dry them well. Place in large bowl and season with pepper flakes. Heat olive oil in a pot or pan until the surface starts to develop a shimmery sheen (but before it starts to smoke). Add salt and then pour hot oil over spinach. Stir vigorously with a fork, coating the spinach until partially wilted.

Place bowl in warmest part of freezer for about an hour and a half. Remove from freezer and stir in fresh chile, lemon zest, and Agrumato. Adjust seasoning. Return to freezer for three-quarters of an hour (or less, if the spinach starts to freeze). Remove from freezer, mix well, and serve immediately on a cold platter, or transfer to refrigerator. If desired, garnish with shaved *bottarga di muggine* (dried gray-mullet roe). ***Serves 4.***

BLUEFISH

Oily, mean, and much maligned: if ever a finny denizen of the sea needed an image consultant, it would be the bluefish. Not only has it been described as an "animated chopping machine" on account of its tendency to overdo it when the dinner bell rings, but detractors claim it tastes "fishy." Taste, though, is subjective, and one man's fishy is another's full flavored. When it's properly cooked the day it's caught, it ranks among the richest, moistest, and most delicious species out there. Given its natural oiliness, the bluefish is a prime candidate for grilling, smoking, and broiling. But counterintuitively, poaching in olive oil works surprisingly well, too. Former Esca chef de cuisine Katie O'Donnell shows how.

Katie O'Donnell's Olive Oil–Poached Bluefish Crostini

FOR THE FISH

1 bluefish fillet (about 8 ounces), skinned

Kosher salt

1 to 2 cups extra-virgin olive oil (or enough to completely cover bluefish)

3 garlic cloves

1 sprig rosemary

FOR THE PICKLED RAMPS

2 cups red wine vinegar

¼ cup water

1 tablespoon sugar

1 teaspoon kosher salt

8 ramps, washed and roots removed

FOR THE CROSTINI

4 slices rustic Italian bread, sliced about ¾ inch thick

Extra-virgin olive oil, for brushing

1 garlic clove

Coarse sea salt, to finish

FOR THE FISH: Preheat oven to 350 degrees. Cut the bluefish into 1-inch pieces and place them in the bottom of a small baking dish. Season with salt and cover completely with olive oil. Add the garlic cloves and rosemary. Cover tightly with foil and cook in the oven for 15 minutes.

FOR THE RAMPS: In a small pot, bring the vinegar, water, sugar, and salt to boil. Submerge ramps and cook until the whites are tender, about 4 to 5 minutes. Remove ramps and reserve pickling liquid for drizzling over crostini. Let ramps cool and cut into 1-inch pieces.

FOR THE CROSTINI: Brush bread with olive oil and grill or toast it. While bread is still hot, rub each slice with the remaining garlic clove. Using a fork or slotted spoon, place an equal portion of the fish atop each slice of bread. Season with coarse sea salt; top each slice equally with the ramps and a drizzle of the pickling liquid. *Serves 4.*

BROCCOLI RABE

Broccoli rabe, that ubiquitous cruciferous *contorno*, is known for its distinctive and delicious bitter taste. But for a fleeting period in the spring, before the new crop comes in, you'll find overwintered bunches that boast a relative sweetness. Use them for this quick and easy recipe from Mario Carbone and Rich Torrisi of New York's Parm, who've masterminded a supermarket-sourced condiment so bafflingly good, it should be a secret weapon in every home cook's arsenal.

Rich Torrisi and Mario Carbone's Spicy Rabe

FOR THE BROCCOLI RABE

1 bunch broccoli rabe (1 to 1½ pounds)

¼ cup extra-virgin olive oil, plus more as needed for cooking

2 garlic cloves, thinly sliced

¼ teaspoon red pepper flakes

Salt, to taste

FOR THE SPICY SAUCE

4 ounces B&G brand hot cherry peppers

2 ounces roasted red peppers

2 ounces crushed tomato

¼ cup olive oil

¼ teaspoon red pepper flakes

¼ teaspoon dried oregano

¼ teaspoon sugar

Salt, to taste

FOR THE BROCCOLI RABE: Pull off any wilted leaves. Cut off any tough or woody stem ends and clean the rabe in cold water. Heat oil in a large pan over medium heat. Add garlic and red pepper flakes to pan, and cook until tender, about a minute or so. Add broccoli rabe, and cook in batches until tender, adding a little water (approximately a tablespoon) and more olive oil as necessary, about 6 to 8 minutes. Season with salt, then remove rabe to a bowl and let cool.

FOR THE SPICY SAUCE: Combine all ingredients in a food processor or blender, and mix until slightly smooth. To serve, toss the rabe with the spicy sauce. *Serves 4 to 6.*

COCONUT MACAROONS

Since Passover is observed by the ritual avoidance of forbidden foods like bread, pasta, bagels, and pizza, the holiday's symbolic flourlessness is usually construed as culinary deprivation. There's another way to look at it: the perfect opportunity to indulge in annual treats like rich, gooey coconut macaroons. This version comes courtesy of pastry chef Deborah Snyder, whose time in New York kitchens like Judson Grill, Union Square Cafe, and Lever House was marked by a focus on homey, often retro desserts. Her recipe could not be simpler, and the results are divine—especially if you deem the "optional" chocolate chunks compulsory.

Deborah Snyder's Coconut Macaroons

3 cups unsweetened desiccated coconut

1½ teaspoons vanilla extract

2 tablespoons plus 1½ teaspoons melted
   unsalted butter

1 cup sugar

3 extra-large or 4 medium-large egg
   whites

1 cup chopped chocolate (optional)

Preheat oven to 350 degrees. In a large mixing bowl, combine coconut, vanilla, butter, and half the sugar. Whip the whites in the bowl of an electric mixer until they begin to get foamy and opaque. Add the remaining sugar in a slow, steady stream and continue whipping until the mixture is pure white and volumized, but just short of holding soft peaks. Fold the whites into the coconut mixture. Add the chocolate, if desired. Using a very small ice-cream scoop or teaspoon, scoop the batter onto parchment-lined cookie sheets, about ½ inch apart. Bake for about 13 to 15 minutes, until lightly browned, turning the tray once during baking. Cool completely. Note: The batter can be made several days in advance, and kept covered and refrigerated. ***Makes about 4 dozen.***

DANDELION GREENS

*P*esky weed to some, seasonal delicacy to others, the jagged, bitter dandelion green is one of those Mediterranean peasant foods newly embraced for their health-giving properties—in this case, a preponderance of iron, calcium, and vitamin A. Delicate young greens are terrific raw in salads, but in the Greek kitchen, the mature leaf is often used in the generic *horta* preparation, (over)boiled and simply dressed with oil and lemon, the way Kefi chef Michael Psilakis's mother made it. Psilakis prefers to preserve the plant's bitter bite by blanching it quickly just to tenderize, then sautéing it with garlic and hot peppers, as in this warm spring salad.

Michael Psilakis's Warm Dandelion Green, Fingerling Potato, and Cherry Pepper Salad

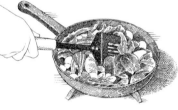

2 bunches mature dandelion greens, washed, thick stems removed

12 pickled cherry peppers

5 tablespoons extra-virgin olive oil, plus more for dressing

6 garlic cloves, crushed and coarsely chopped

18 fingerling potatoes, roasted and peeled

1½ cups pitted Thassos olives (Kalamata may be substituted)

Juice of 3 lemons

1½ cups crumbled Greek feta cheese

Salt and freshly ground black pepper

Add dandelion greens to a large pot of boiling salted water and cook just until the midribs (the part of the stem that extends into the leaf) are malleable. Immediately remove and shock in an ice bath. Lay greens on a dish towel to dry thoroughly. Stem and quarter the cherry peppers, discarding the seeds if a milder degree of heat is desired. Add 5 tablespoons extra-virgin olive oil to a large pan over medium heat. In rapid succession, cook garlic and peppers until garlic begins to brown, add potatoes and stir to coat with oil, add dandelion greens and olives to warm, and deglaze with lemon juice, giving the pan's contents a quick toss. Take care not to overcook the greens and potatoes. Transfer to a large serving bowl and add crumbled feta. Dress with olive oil and season to taste. ***Serves 4.***

EGGS

Just like Easter Peeps, eggs have a season. Of course, you can get them year-round just about anywhere, but egg-laying officially begins in spring, when chickens—naturally prompted by increasing daylight—bump up their production cycle. Connoisseurs say that eggs from contented, pasture-raised hens are tastier—with brighter yolks and more delicate whites—not to mention much more nutritious than the factory-farmed variety. For a preparation worthy of truly farm-fresh specimens, consider this recipe from George Weld, reigning grill-maestro at Williamsburg, Brooklyn's, best breakfast joint, the aptly named Egg. (In case you're wondering, Mark Rothko was Weld's landlord's great-uncle.)

George Weld's Eggs Rothko

2 tablespoons unsalted butter

2 thick slices of brioche or challah

2 large or extra-large eggs

1 cup grated good-quality
    Cheddar cheese like
    Grafton

Place oven rack in lowest position and preheat oven to broil. Melt 1 tablespoon of butter in a large skillet over medium heat until it begins to foam. Place brioche slices in the skillet, moving them around until well buttered and browned. Using a biscuit cutter or drinking glass, press a hole in the center of each bread slice and discard the cutout rounds. Divide the remaining tablespoon of butter between the 2 holes in the bread. When butter begins to foam, crack an egg into each hole and cook until the egg whites set about halfway up the sides of the yolks. Flip the bread with a spatula and cook for another minute or so. Remove bread from skillet and place onto a broiler pan. Spread grated cheese thoroughly over the bread, covering as much surface area as possible to prevent the bread from burning, and place pan under the broiler. Remove as soon as the cheese is melted. Serve with broiled tomatoes or a simply dressed green salad. *Serves 2.*

STINGING NETTLES

Prized by foragers, seasonally minded cooks, and, according to some people, anyone who suffers from anemia, baldness, eczema, sinusitis, or gout, the wild stinging nettle has a whiff of danger about it. Upon contact, tiny needles release chemicals that cause skin irritation, which is why you need gloves to handle them. But not to worry. Cooking renders the tender leaves harmless, and, as you'll see in this recipe from Dan Drohan, who heads the kitchen at Otto Enoteca e Pizzeria, quite delicious.

Dan Drohan's Fettuccine with Nettles and Lemon

6 ounces stinging-nettle leaves

Salt

1 pound fettuccine (or spaghetti, linguine, or bucatini)

2 tablespoons extra-virgin olive oil, plus more to finish

2 garlic cloves, thinly sliced

1 teaspoon freshly ground black pepper

Pinch of crushed red pepper flakes

Zest and juice of 1 lemon

2½ tablespoons mascarpone cheese

2 tablespoons Parmigiano-Reggiano cheese

While wearing gloves, pick off the nettle leaves and discard the tough stems. In a pot, blanch the nettles in boiling salted water and drain. Roughly chop the nettles and reserve. In a large pot, bring 8 quarts of salted water to a boil and cook pasta until al dente. While the pasta is cooking, heat 2 tablespoons of the olive oil in a large sauté pan over medium heat. Add garlic, black pepper, and red pepper flakes and cook until the garlic is golden brown. Add the chopped nettles to the pan and toss with the garlic until the nettles are warm. Add half of the lemon juice, and remove the pan from the heat. Stir in the mascarpone and half of the lemon zest with the nettles mixture. Finish cooking the pasta, reserving a little of the cooking water, and drain. Return the sauté pan to the burner over medium heat. Add the pasta and toss with the reserved pasta water and the nettles mixture. Adjust seasoning with the remaining lemon juice and zest, and more black pepper. Finish with the Parmigiano-Reggiano and olive oil. *Serves 4.*

STRAWBERRIES

*L*ocal strawberries begin perfuming farmers' markets with their intoxicating fragrance in spring, and only grow sweeter as the season progresses. Dipped in sugar and a little crème fraîche, they are just about perfect. That you knew. But have you ever wondered what they'd taste like run through the blender and transformed into gazpacho? Eleven Madison Park's Daniel Humm has. He volunteers the following recipe. And we offer a handy hulling tip that requires nothing more than a sturdy drinking straw and a little wrist action.

Daniel Humm's Strawberry Gazpacho

FOR THE TOAST

2 slices of country white bread

1 tablespoon extra-virgin olive oil

1 garlic clove, crushed

1 sprig thyme

FOR THE GAZPACHO

1½ pounds strawberries, plus 8 pieces
   for garnish

1 red bell pepper, cored and seeded

½ green bell pepper, cored and seeded

2 cucumbers, peeled and seeded

1 garlic clove

3 ounces tomato juice

3 tablespoons red wine vinegar

2 tablespoons extra-virgin olive oil

Sea salt to taste

Tabasco to taste

GARNISH

1 tablespoon extra-virgin olive oil

Freshly ground black pepper to taste

4 basil leaves

FOR THE TOAST: In a small pan over medium-low heat, toast the bread in the olive oil with the crushed garlic and thyme until golden brown. Reserve.

FOR THE GAZPACHO: Hull the strawberries by inserting a straw at the bottom of the berry and pushing it through the cap. Dice the berries, peppers, cucumbers, and garlic and combine with tomato juice, vinegar, and olive oil. Let marinate for 3 hours at room temperature. Combine all ingredients, including the toasted bread, in a blender, and blend until smooth. Strain through chinois (optional). Season with salt and Tabasco. Finish with olive oil, black pepper, and basil and garnish with the reserved strawberries. *Serves 4 to 6.*

WHITE ASPARAGUS

No point in arguing food miles to certain European expat chefs when the subject turns to (nonlocal) white asparagus. So revered are the oversize albino stalks in Germany, for example, that during asparagus season (or Spargelzeit), there are Oktoberfest-level celebrations, peeling contests, and, in a few asparagus-crazed towns, the crowning of an asparagus king and queen. Kurt Gutenbrunner, the Austrian chef/owner of Blaue Gans and Wallsé whose unbridled enthusiasm for the prized veggie makes you wonder whether he's descended from asparagus royalty himself, recommends the imported French variety available at specialty grocers. He also suggests "eating a great deal of them as the season is short."

Kurt Gutenbrunner's White Asparagus

3 pounds (about 16 pieces) white
    asparagus
1½ tablespoons salt

1 tablespoon sugar
4 tablespoons unsalted butter
1 small piece of baguette or white bread

Drape a dish towel over a large, inverted mixing bowl. To peel asparagus, grip the spear with three fingers, protecting the tip, and lean it against the bowl to prevent it from breaking. With a swivel vegetable peeler, remove the thick outer layer starting just below the tip, turning the spear as you peel. Peel them well, as the skin can be tough and bitter. Trim approximately 1 inch off the woody end of each spear. Add the salt, sugar, and butter to 4 quarts of water in a large pot and bring to a boil. Add the bread, which helps eliminate bitterness, and the asparagus, and cook for about 8 minutes, until cooked through but still firm. Remove asparagus and dry on a towel. Serve at room temperature with an herb vinaigrette (made with good extra-virgin olive oil and lemon juice) or hollandaise sauce. *Serves 4.*

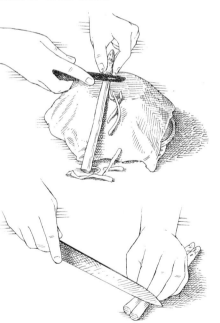

Summer is one of my favorite times to eat simply. And to appreciate the summer's bounty is to cook things, or not cook if you are really sage, as they reach the peak of their potential and bloom in maximum flavor.

I'm always on the hunt for *primizie*: the very first piece of produce of a new season. As a chef, I have to embrace each vegetable at its freshest but I also appreciate not just any strawberry, but the sweetest strawberry with the maximum acid/sweetness balance. In February, we often keep the same dish on the specials for four weeks at a crack. In July, to do so would be a disservice to our local farms, to the ingredients, and, most important, to their flavors.

During the summer, you have to map out the harvest in order to make best use of fruits and vegetables during their short windows of opportunity. In April, we obsess over ramps. At Otto, we use ramps in farro and pasta and on pizza. A few weeks later, asparagus is at its peak. In the heat of summer, I love technicolor chard and spicy arugula, both raw and simply dressed with extra-virgin olive oil and lemon. I love sweet white eggplants, Romanesco, and sweet pattypan squash to shave paper thin and serve raw in a salad.

On the East Coast, nearly all of our local planted produce is harvested during the summer and fall. By July Fourth, our gardens are beautiful and lush. But our local fruit, vegetables, and herbs don't all deliver at once and they are not all available throughout the entire season. Raspberries come and go, then peaches come and stay a while, but we own neither for very long.

Each perfect specimen is available for a fleeting moment. Use them each quickly, then move on. And don't forget to hold out for that last week of August and into September for a perfect ripe heirloom tomato, served just cut from the vine with torn basil leaves and some freshly ground black pepper. Summer lives year round in my mind but is evanescent on the vine.

—MARIO BATALI

SUMMER

BLACK MINT

Black mint isn't an herb gone goth, but rather a type of peppermint that's commonly used for tea and actually turns out to have more of a dark-purplish or brownish cast around the stem. As the opening pastry chef at A Voce—before landing her current position at a Gray Kunz property in Hong Kong—April Robinson featured the hardy perennial in a wonderfully refreshing *granité* that she used to garnish season-bridging Black Mission figs.

April Robinson's Black-Mint Granité

¼ cup black mint leaves, washed and stemmed

1 cup milk

¼ cup sugar

Juice of 1 lemon

Crush mint by stacking and rolling up the leaves and mashing them with the back of a knife. Combine milk and mint in a pot over medium heat, and bring almost to a boil. Remove pot from heat and add sugar, allowing it to dissolve. Cover with plastic wrap and allow liquid to cool completely. Strain through a fine-mesh strainer, add lemon juice, and pour into a shallow metal pan. Freeze, breaking up the ice with the back of a spoon after the first 2 hours and then every hour or so. Shave the *granité* with a fork over each portion of roasted figs.

FOR FIGS

15 small-medium Black Mission figs

Zest of 1 orange, pith removed

¾ cup orange juice

2 strips lemon peel

1 tablespoon lemon juice

1 star anise, toasted

1½ tablespoons honey

2 tablespoons Green Chartreuse

Preheat oven to 400 degrees. Cut the tips off the figs. Combine all ingredients and toss in a bowl. Stand figs up in a shallow baking dish and cover with aluminum foil. Bake until plump and soft, but not split (approximately 20 to 25 minutes). Let cool in pan, preferably overnight in fridge. When ready to serve, slice figs in half lengthwise and warm slightly in a small saucepan with a little roasting liquid over medium heat. Reduce the remaining roasting liquid in a saucepan over medium heat to syrup consistency, about 8 minutes, and drizzle over figs. Divide into 5 bowls, top with *granité*, and sprinkle each serving with a couple of drops of Chartreuse. ***Serves 5.***

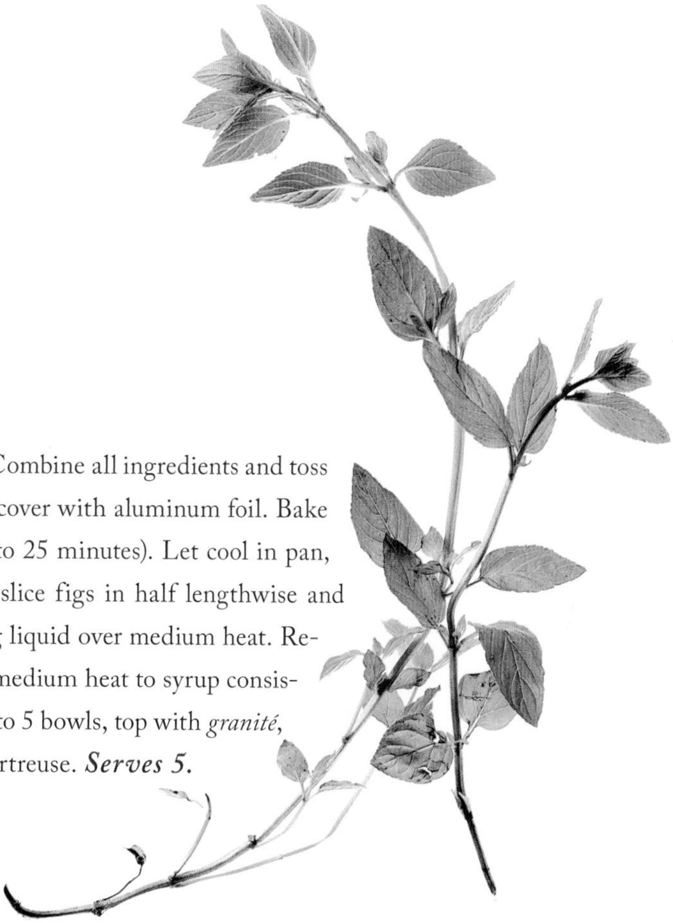

FAVA BEANS

*I*f snap peas are the definition of gustatory ease, favas—with their imposing pods and skins that restaurant prep cooks spend resentful hours peeling—are their polar opposite. Except, that is, if you follow this liberating recipe from Ignacio Mattos, who picked it up from Mexican members of his kitchen crew while he was the chef at Manhattan's Il Buco. If young and tender enough, favas can be grilled and consumed whole—pods, skins, and all (except for that fibrous string that holds it all together).

Ignacio Mattos's Grilled Favas

1 pound fresh fava beans in their pods (the younger the better)

1 teaspoon fleur de sel

1 teaspoon ground chile pepper

1 teaspoon picked rosemary

3 or 4 cloves garlic, chopped

¼ cup extra-virgin olive oil, plus more to finish

2 tablespoons water

Juice of 1 lemon

7 or 8 canned anchovies, in oil

Handful of toasted bread crumbs

Preheat the grill to medium. In a large bowl, mix together the beans, fleur de sel, chile pepper, rosemary, garlic, oil, and water. Toss to coat the fava pods, then place them on the grill over medium heat. Grill favas for several minutes, until charred, then flip them over and char the other side, cooking until the pods seem about to open. Remove pods from the grill, return them to the mixing bowl, and squeeze the lemon over them. Toss the pods to coat. Check the seasoning, and add salt if necessary. Chop the anchovies and add them to the bowl, mixing well. Place the pods on a serving platter, drizzle to taste with olive oil, and sprinkle the bread crumbs on top. Serve hot or at room temperature, with steak or whole grilled fish. *Serves 4.*

SUMMER FLOUNDER

*P*lump and firm-fleshed, the summer flounder—aka fluke—takes its name from the fact that it swims inshore during warmer months and fins it back out to deeper waters in the winter. Most fluke weigh in at about four pounds, but the substantial specimen you see pictured tipped the scales at three times that. Old salts call these jumbos "doormats" because of their shape and size and the fact that they lie on the ocean floor with their eyes (both located on the left side) protruding upward. Grilling or roasting a fluke whole is the best way to retain all the delicate flavor from the bones. But this fish is good enough to eat as sashimi, or, as John Fraser of New York's Dovetail prepares it, filleted and quickly grilled on one side, then splashed about in a vinaigrette.

John Fraser's Fluke Escabèche

¼ cup extra-virgin olive oil, plus more
    for fish
Juice of 2 limes
½ teaspoon crushed red pepper flakes
Sea salt

Freshly ground white pepper
2 tablespoons chopped fresh oregano
½ red onion, diced
1 pound fluke fillet
1 large avocado, diced

Whisk together olive oil, lime juice, red pepper, a pinch of sea salt, a pinch of white pepper oregano, and onion. Season fluke with salt and white pepper and rub generously with olive oil. Grill fluke on one side over very high heat in a stovetop grill pan or on an outdoor grill. Cook until it becomes slightly translucent, approximately 3 to 4 minutes. Remove from heat and let rest for a minute. Add fillet to the vinaigrette and marinate for 5 minutes. Remove fillet and slice into 1-inch strips. Add avocado to vinaigrette and spoon over sliced fluke. Toss lightly and serve warm. *Serves 4.*

HARDNECK GARLIC

Harvested in July and August and then cured for several weeks, hardneck garlic is at its pungent peak in late summer and early fall. Unlike the supermarket softneck variety, hardneck is difficult to grow, but it yields bigger and easier-to-peel cloves that possess superior flavor. Look for the woody-stemmed bulbs at farmers' markets, and showcase them in this confit garlic recipe from chef Ryan Tate, who did time at New York's trendsetting locavore restaurant Savoy.

Ryan Tate's Confit Hardneck Garlic

1 head of hardneck garlic

Pinch of kosher salt

1 sprig rosemary

2 sprigs thyme

1 *chile de árbol*

1 cup extra-virgin olive oil

2 oil-cured olives, finely chopped

Zest of 1 lemon

1 tablespoon chopped fresh
   tarragon leaves

Preheat oven to 300 degrees. Cut garlic bulb in half horizontally. Sprinkle with salt. Place bulbs in small ovenproof dish (or place each half-bulb in a small ramekin), and arrange the rosemary, thyme, and chile around the garlic. Pour olive oil to completely cover garlic. Bake in oven for 50 minutes or until garlic is tender. Remove from the oven and allow garlic to reach room temperature. Remove garlic from oil, keeping the shape of the half-bulbs intact. Place on a serving plate and sprinkle with the chopped olives, lemon zest, and tarragon leaves. Drizzle with a little of the garlic oil, and spread onto crackers or toast.
Serves 2 to 4.

HATCH CHILE PEPPERS

Gilroy has its garlic, and Castroville its artichokes, but no one stakes a stronger claim to green chile peppers than Hatch, New Mexico, the self-proclaimed Chile Capital of the World. Before she closed her pioneering Manhattan shop Kitchen/Market, chef Dona Abramson would import shipments of "Big Jim" New Mexican peppers straight from the source for a few weeks each year, to the capsaicin-craving delight of New Mexican expats and chile-heads alike. Delicious combined with tomatillos in salsa or scrambled with eggs, the long, meaty peppers can also be stuffed and baked, which is how Abramson prepares them here.

Dona Abramson's Hatch Green Chiles Rellenos

¼ to ½ cup pepitas (hulled pumpkin
  seeds)

4 Hatch green chiles (the straighter, the
  better)

1 large ear of corn

1 small yellow onion, diced

Olive or canola oil

Kosher salt

½ to ¾ cup grated Chihuahua cheese
  (Monterey Jack may be substituted)

¼ cup grated Cotija cheese

¼ cup chopped cilantro

Watercress and tomato sauce,
  for serving

Preheat oven to 350 degrees. Toast pepitas in a dry skillet over medium heat, stirring frequently, until they start to brown. Roast chiles directly over an open flame (grill or stovetop) until skin is blackened and blistered on both sides. Place in a bowl and cover with a plate or plastic wrap to help steam off skin. When cool, gently peel by hand or with the back of a knife. Slit chiles from stem to tip and carefully remove seeds. Set aside. Slice kernels from the corn cob and sauté them with onions in oil until soft. Season to taste and let cool. Combine cheeses, corn mixture, toasted pepitas, and chopped cilantro. Check seasoning. Form mixture into four "logs" and place in the chiles. Close "seam" as tightly as possible, with toothpicks if necessary. Bake on an oiled and salted baking pan or casserole dish until cheese begins to melt. Serve over watercress with cooked or raw tomato sauce. If desired, diced and roasted squash may be added to the stuffing. *Serves 4.*

HEIRLOOM TOMATOES

*I*n the Northeast, two of summer's sweetest pleasures arrive as it's ending: an ocean warm enough to swim in, and exquisitely ripe heirloom tomatoes. Frank Falcinelli, co-owner of Frankies 457 Court Street Spuntino in Brooklyn, has been known to mainline them for lunch in a salad so simple it barely requires a recipe. The combination of ingredients is unexpected and their quality, paramount: The tomato must be super-sweet and brightly acidic (look for varieties like Cherokee Purple, Brandywine, and Aunt Ruby's German Green). The avocado should be lush and ripe; the sea salt, coarse-grained and minimally processed; the olive oil, extra-virgin and, says the chef, preferably Sicilian. The basic premise is to add salinity to the acidity of the tomatoes, or, as Falcinelli puts it, "to make gazpacho in my mouth."

Frank Falcinelli's Heirloom Tomato and Avocado Salad

1 perfectly ripe medium or ½ large heirloom tomato	A quarter of a red onion
Half an avocado	Coarse sea salt
	2 to 3 ounces extra-virgin olive oil

Wash, core, and slice the tomato in thin wedges. Seed the avocado, and with a teaspoon turn out little scoops on top of tomatoes. Slice onion against the grain and add to salad. Sprinkle with salt and drizzle with oil. Falcinelli recommends shaving Montasio cheese over the salad for variety, and having enough crusty bread on hand to sop up the delicious dregs. ***Serves 1.***

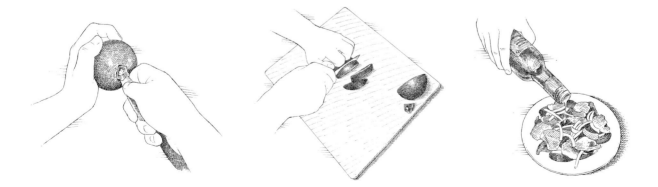

"REGULAR" TOMATOES

*L*umpy, misshapen heirloom tomatoes have such a monopoly on the imagination of the typical farmers' market shopper that to traffic in red, round, generic-seeming hybrids requires a bit of salesmanship. Take, for instance, the sign we once spotted at a Union Square Greenmarket farmstand that read "REGULAR TOMATOES." It went on to explain, in so many words, that although these tomatoes aren't heirlooms, they're not half bad—in fact, they're perfectly vine-ripened, sweet and juicy, and, typically, half the cost of the average Brandywine or Green Zebra. To prove this thesis, bring a bunch home and showcase them in a terrific BLT, created by Tien Ho when he ran the kitchen at Momofuku Ssäm Bar.

Tien Ho's BLT with Spicy Mayo

1 cup Kewpie mayonnaise

1 tablespoon Sriracha sauce

16 slices of Burgers' jowl "bacon" (available at smokehouse.com), or substitute your own favorite

½ medium onion, diced

2 tablespoons olive oil, plus more for bread and tomatoes

½ head iceberg lettuce, sliced into ½-inch strips

Salt and freshly ground black pepper to taste

4 (½-inch-thick) slices of good Italian bread

4 beefsteak tomatoes, cored and sliced

Preheat oven to 350 degrees. Make the spicy mayonnaise by mixing Kewpie mayonnaise with Sriracha. Reserve cold. On a large baking sheet, cook bacon in the oven to desired crispness. Reserve warm. In a large sauté pan, sweat onions in olive oil until tender. Add lettuce and season with salt and pepper. Lightly cook through and reserve warm. Brush bread with olive oil and grill on both sides. Season with salt and pepper. Spread spicy mayo over grilled bread. Top with sautéed lettuce-onion mix and slices of tomato. Season tomatoes with salt, pepper, and olive oil. Finish with bacon. *Serves 2.*

KIRBY CUCUMBERS

Short and squat, with a warty complexion, the Kirby may be the ugly duckling of the cucumber world, but it's also the best for pickling—and when it comes down to it, aside from being sliced and tossed into a Pimm's Cup, isn't pickledom the highest office to which a cucumber can aspire? Find them near their slender, smooth-skinned cousins at just about every other farmers' market stand throughout the summer, and then try them in this recipe from Ed McFarland of Ed's Lobster Bar.

Ed McFarland's Pickles

6 small Kirby cucumbers

4 cups water

1 cup pickling or kosher salt

¾ cup sugar

4 habañero peppers

2 cups red wine vinegar

2 garlic cloves, peeled and crushed

⅛ teaspoon whole black peppercorns

½ teaspoon celery seed

¾ teaspoon coriander

1 allspice berry

¾ teaspoon mustard seed

For the brine, using a knife or, preferably, a mandoline, slice the cucumbers approximately ⅛ inch thick. In a large nonreactive bowl or plastic container, mix the water, salt, and ¼ cup of the sugar with a whisk. Add the cucumber slices and the whole peppers to the mixture, thoroughly covering them with the brine. Cover container and let stand for 12 hours. Remove cucumber slices and peppers from brine and rinse well with cold water. For the pickling mix, combine the remaining ½ cup sugar, vinegar, garlic, and spices in another nonreactive bowl or plastic container. Add the cucumber slices and peppers. Cover and refrigerate for 5 hours before serving. Pickles should last refrigerated up to 60 days.

SANTA ROSA PLUMS

*T*angy, flavorful Santa Rosa plums proliferate in Northern California, where they were first bred more than a century ago by horticulturist Luther Burbank, and where Abraço chef/partner Elizabeth Quijada grew up. Although they once represented a third of the state's plum crop, they've been surpassed in recent years by larger, often blander varieties, destined for shipping and the commercial market. Your best bet for locating a ripe, juicy specimen is a farmers' market. Try them in Quijada's simple tart, which calls for poaching the fruit and candying the skin to use as an edible garnish.

Elizabeth Quijada's Poached Santa Rosa Plum Tart

FOR *PÂTE SUCRÉE* TART SHELL

1¼ cups organic flour

⅓ cup organic sugar

¾ cup (1½ sticks) organic unsalted butter, plus more, melted, for pan

Pinch of salt

2 egg yolks

½ teaspoon organic vanilla extract

FOR TART

½ cup sugar (Quijada uses Florida Crystals organic cane sugar)

4 Santa Rosa plums

Superfine sugar, for dusting (or finely ground Florida Crystals)

FOR TART SHELL: In a mixer, or with clean hands, work together flour, sugar, butter, and salt until butter is incorporated and the texture resembles coarse cornmeal. Form a well in the center of the flour-butter mixture, add the egg yolks and vanilla, and with a fork combine ingredients starting in the middle and working outward until all is uniform. The dough should be soft; if it is sticky, add a bit more flour.

Line the bottom of a rectangular 4-by-14-inch tart pan with parchment and brush with melted butter. Press dough in pan evenly. Prick the bottom of the tart with a fork and refrigerate for 30 minutes. Bake at 325 degrees until firm, but not brown, about 12 to 15 minutes.

FOR TART: Preheat oven to 300 degrees. Make simple syrup by combining the sugar with 2 cups boiling water, stirring well to dissolve. Cut the plums in half from stem to bottom, twist halves to separate, remove the pits, place skin side down in a skillet, and cover with simple syrup. Poach over medium-low heat until tender, approximately 6 or 7 minutes. Let cool for a few minutes, then remove gently onto a plate. Carefully remove the plum skins, keeping them intact, and lay on a parchment-lined baking sheet. Spread each skin flat and sprinkle with superfine sugar. Bake at 300 for about 6 minutes, until they start to harden, then flip skins and sprinkle the opposite sides with sugar. Continue baking for another 6 minutes. Remove from oven and let cool, and raise oven temperature to 350. Slice each half-plum into moons and fan over the baked tart shell. Sprinkle top with sugar and bake for 10 minutes. When cool, remove from pan and cut into slices, topping each with a piece of candied skin. *Serves 4 to 6.*

SPEARMINT

*L*eNell Smothers, who used to run the charmingly quirky LeNell's liquor store in Red Hook, Brooklyn, is a born-and-bred Southerner (and, not incidentally, a bourbon booster and julep lover). A few years ago, on the occasion of the annual running of the Kentucky Derby, she shared a mint julep recipe, but by no means the definitive one—which, according to Smothers, who has written a scholarly treatise on the subject, does not exist. "Juleps were a farmer's drink," she says. They've been made, over time, with rum, brandy, and rye, and consumed by many a Colonial settler for breakfast. Regarding the mint, there are those who muddle and those who don't; Smothers does. You can find spearmint (milder in flavor than peppermint) throughout the year, but look for it at farmers' markets during the summer months when the herb is at its peak. Or grow your own like Smothers used to do in an old clawfoot bathtub outside her shop.

LeNell Smothers's Granny's Whiskey Julep

1 teaspoon Granny's Not So Simple
    Syrup (below) (or Pedro Ximénez
    cream sherry)
2 dashes Fee Brothers whiskey barrel-
    aged bitters

5 spearmint leaves
2 ounces 100-proof bourbon or rye
Splash of Prichard's Tennessee rum
Spearmint sprigs
Confectioners' sugar (optional)

Add simple syrup, bitters, and mint leaves to a silver julep cup or well-chilled double old-fashioned glass. Gently muddle the leaves with the syrup and bitters without overly bruising the mint. Remove leaves from syrup and discard. Add crushed ice to fill about ¾ of the cup. Pour in bourbon or rye. Stir until frost forms on outside of glass. Add more ice to form a mound above the rim of the cup. Top with a healthy splash of rum. Insert sprigs of mint along the side of the cup. Cut a straw so that it rises about an inch or two above the ice when inserted fully into the cup, and place it into the mint sprigs. Dust the top with confectioners' sugar if desired. ***Makes 1 drink.***

GRANNY'S NOT SO SIMPLE SYRUP: Add 1 pound of golden raisins to a quart jar. Cover with gin. Let sit for about 2 weeks.

NASTURTIUMS

Much more than a beautiful garnish, nasturtiums make for eminent nose-to-tail (stem-to-petal?) eating. The flowers, leaves, and stems add a nice peppery touch to everything from soups to salads. You can even pickle the seedpods and use them as a substitute for capers, should you be so inclined. Although Annie Wayte, the English-born chef late of Nicole's and 202, doesn't go that far, she does use the chopped leaves and blossoms for nasturtium mayonnaise—her chosen condiment for crab salad—and, yes, she recommends reserving a few flowers for garnish.

Annie Wayte's Nasturtium Blossom Mayonnaise

12 nasturtium blossoms with leaves, plus
   3 whole blossoms for garnish
1 garlic clove
1 teaspoon sea salt
1 egg yolk

½ cup extra-virgin olive oil
¼ cup sunflower or vegetable oil
Juice of 1 lemon
Salt and pepper to taste

Coarsely chop nasturtium blossoms and leaves. Mash garlic with sea salt, preferably in a mortar. Add egg yolk and mix thoroughly. Combine oils and slowly trickle them into egg mixture a few drops at a time, whisking vigorously until emulsified. If mayonnaise becomes too thick, thin it with a drop or two of lemon juice, and continue mixing until all the oil has been added. Stir in chopped nasturtiums. Adjust seasoning and consistency with salt, pepper, and lemon juice. Serving suggestion: Place alongside picked jumbo crabmeat, radishes, baby fennel, and cooked new potatoes arranged as a salad with toasted country bread. ***Makes approximately ¾ cup.***

PANISSE LETTUCE

*P*retty enough to be a table centerpiece, this frilly lime-green lettuce has palate appeal, too. A new selection of green oak leaf, panisse has tender but sturdy-enough leaves and a bittersweet flavor that fairly cries out for a zingy dressing like the pistachio vinaigrette Dan Kluger concocted over at New York City's ABC Kitchen. His fresh-herb-and-chile–enhanced supersalad is something you'll want to eat all summer long.

Dan Kluger's Panisse Lettuce with Pistachio Vinaigrette

FOR THE DRESSING

½ cup extra-virgin olive oil

¼ cup plus 2 tablespoons raw pistachios

½ Thai chile, seeded and minced

4 teaspoons lemon juice

3 tablespoons Champagne vinegar

1 teaspoon kosher salt

½ teaspoon freshly ground black pepper

FOR THE SALAD

2 heads panisse lettuce (or substitute
    butterhead lettuce)

2 tablespoons finely chopped chives

2 tablespoons finely chopped oregano

2 tablespoons finely chopped mint

2 tablespoons finely chopped tarragon

8 French breakfast radishes, thinly sliced
    into rounds

½ cup Sevillano or Manzanilla olives,
    pitted and chopped

FOR THE DRESSING: In a small pot, heat olive oil and pistachios together over a low flame until warm. Place warm pistachios in food processor and pulse until roughly chopped. Immediately pour pistachio mixture into a bowl with Thai chile and let sit for 10 minutes. Add lemon juice, Champagne vinegar, kosher salt, and ground pepper.

FOR THE SALAD: Trim stem and remove outside leaves of each lettuce head. Cut each lettuce in half lengthwise and wash. Combine herbs with the pistachio vinaigrette. Place each half lettuce in a separate bowl and spoon an equal amount of vinaigrette on top of each serving. Sprinkle each with radishes and olives, and finish with freshly ground pepper. *Serves 4.*

PARSLEY

*P*arsley, the perennial garnish, gets to shine in tabbouleh, the Middle Eastern salad whose parsley content, according to Ilili chef-owner Philippe Massoud, corresponds directly to a country's water supply. Nowhere is it greener, he says, than in his native Lebanon, where grains of bulgur in a typical tabbouleh are few and far between. The crucial steps are drying the herb completely and stemming it well. "We are the only restaurant I know of that serves leaf-only parsley," says Massoud. "It's costly, but it's worth it." Be sure to use flat-leaf, which tastes parsley-er, so to speak, than the curly variety.

Philippe Massoud's Tabbouleh

6 bunches Italian (flat-leaf) parsley

1 bunch mint

1 large or 2 small heirloom tomatoes (enough to yield 2 cups)

1 large Spanish onion

1 cup fresh (about 6 lemons) lemon juice

1 cup extra-virgin olive oil

Salt and freshly ground black pepper to taste

Pinch of allspice

1 cup bulgur, uncooked

2 heads romaine lettuce (to yield 16 inner leaves
   from the heart)

Pick the parsley leaves from the stems, wash thoroughly, and spin in a salad spinner to dry. Spread leaves on a tray and let air-dry completely. Pick, wash, and dry mint leaves in the same way. Using a sharp knife, chiffonade the parsley and crosscut three times, to yield 4 cups. Chiffonade the mint to yield ½ cup. Core and seed the tomato, and cut in ¼-inch dice to yield 2 cups. Finely dice the onion to yield ½ cup. Combine the lemon juice, olive oil, salt, pepper, and allspice in a small Tupperware container. Seal, and shake well to blend. Wash bulgur thoroughly until the water runs clear. Strain and squeeze to re-move all excess water. Clean romaine thoroughly, peeling away outer leaves to expose the heart and slicing off the top 2 (greenest) inches. In a mixing bowl, combine the parsley, mint, 1½ cups of diced tomato, onion, and bulgur. Gently mix with a spoon to incorporate the ingredients, being careful not to bruise them. Add the dressing and mix again. Place mixture in a serving bowl and arrange the romaine-heart leaves around the perimeter. Garnish with remaining tomato. Use the romaine leaves as edible utensils. *Serves 4 to 6.*

PEACHES

Is there any fruit as peachy as a peach? Its color, its sweetness, its outrageous juiciness cannot be beat. The only problem with peaches is finding ones that live up to their potential. Look for those that are bruise-free and firm but that give slightly to a gentle tweak. A deep, intoxicating fragrance means they're good and ripe. If you can restrain yourself from devouring them over the sink, bake them in a pie, drop a slice or two into a glass of wine, or try this sweet-and-spicy treatment from pastry chef Charmaine McFarlane, who created the recipe for the Shop at Andaz 5th Avenue in New York.

Charmaine McFarlane's Peaches with Chiles, Sugar, Salt, and Lime

6 tablespoons sugar

2 tablespoons kosher salt

2 Thai chiles, chopped

2 limes

6 peaches

Vanilla ice cream, for serving

Combine the sugar, salt, and chopped chiles in a mortar and pestle and grind to a consistency like wet sand. Zest the limes and reserve the fruit for another use. Stir zest into the sugar mixture. Halve the peaches by slicing them along their seams and cutting through to the pits and around the fruit. Gently twist until the halves separate. Remove pits. Blanch the peach halves for 45 seconds and remove to an ice bath for a minute. Peel off the skins. Sprinkle peaches with the sugar mixture and let macerate for half an hour. Serve with vanilla ice cream. *Serves 4 to 6*.

PIMIENTOS DE PADRÓN

Stubby *pimientos de Padrón* are a specialty of Galicia, Spain. In recent years, they and their Asian-cultivar ilk, like *shishito*s and *fushimi*s, have become just as popular in the tapas bars of New York City. Blistered in hot oil and generously salted, as prepared by Tertulia chef Seamus Mullen, they make a tasty, and sometimes surprising, snack: one in ten can be quite spicy, they say; late-season peppers, harvested in September and October, can be even hotter.

Seamus Mullen's Pimientos de Padrón

2 tablespoons olive oil

½ pound *pimientos de Padrón,* washed and dried well

Maldon sea salt

Sherry vinegar (optional)

Heat the oil in a sauté pan until smoking hot. Sauté peppers until they blister, approximately 1 minute, turning them over to cook all sides. Remove and drain on a paper towel. Sprinkle with Maldon sea salt and serve. For a more piquant bite, add a splash of sherry vinegar. ***Serves 4.***

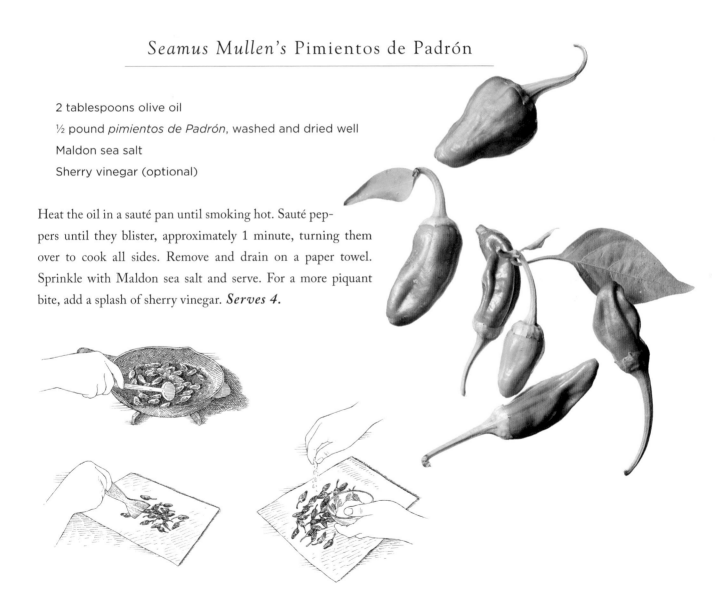

PURPLE EGGPLANT

Although it's low in calories, when cooked in oil, eggplant absorbs fat like a sumo wrestler at an all-you-can-eat buffet. (And therein, in large part, lies its appeal.) From late summer through early fall, look for a multitude of smooth-skinned specimens, including the slim, pale-purple Chinese eggplant and the short, squat, heirloom Italian variety called Rosa Bianco. Tanoreen chef-owner Rawia Bishara (who is to fried eggplant what Joël Robuchon is to mashed potatoes) recommends the standard purple American variety known as Globe for her vegetarian *musaka'a* (not to be confused with the meat-and-béchamel-larded Greek moussaka).

Rawia Bishara's Eggplant Musaka'a

4 large eggplants, peeled and cut into
    2-inch cubes

Salt as needed

1¼ cups olive oil

2 large Spanish onions, peeled and
    chopped

1 jalapeño, seeded and minced

6 garlic cloves, chopped

1 tablespoon cumin

1 teaspoon ground coriander

1 teaspoon freshly ground black
    pepper

12 large plum tomatoes, cut into small
    cubes

1 cup canned chickpeas, drained

Juice of 1 lemon

Sprinkle the eggplant cubes with salt to draw out moisture and let stand in a colander for 30 minutes. Rinse the eggplant to remove salt and then pat dry with a paper towel. In a large pan, fry the eggplant in 1 cup of the olive oil over high heat for approximately 2 to 3 minutes on each side or until golden brown.

The eggplant will absorb most of the oil. Remove from the pan with a slotted spoon, set aside on paper towels to absorb excess oil, and discard any leftover oil. (As an alternative to frying, brush the eggplant with oil and bake at 400 degrees for 15 minutes.) Add the remaining ¼ cup olive oil to the pan and add the onions. Sauté onions until caramelized, then stir in the jalapeño and garlic. Sauté for 3 minutes, then add cumin, coriander, ½ teaspoon salt, and pepper. Once you have smelled the aroma of the garlic and spices, add the tomatoes, chickpeas, lemon juice, and half a cup of water. Bring liquid to a boil and then simmer for 3 minutes. Add eggplant and fold once into sauce. Bring mixture to boil and then simmer for 10 minutes at lowest temperature. Serve hot, at room temperature, or cold. ***Serves 8.***

THAI CHILES

As a general rule, the smaller the chile, the hotter its bite. That's why you can count on these tiny capsicums, also known as bird or bird's-eye chiles, to pack an outsize punch. Look for them in Asian specialty produce stores and also farmers' markets in late summer and early fall. Barehanded and undaunted, King Phojanakong, the chef of what may be New York's only Thai-Filipino restaurants, Kuma Inn and Umi Nom, pummels them into submission for the toothsome condiment he serves with sautéed Chinese sausage and sticky rice, but there's no shame in wearing gloves and protective goggles.

King Phojanakong's Thai Chile–Lime Sauce

8 to 10 Thai chiles
2 garlic cloves
1 tablespoon palm sugar
2 tablespoons fresh lime juice
1 tablespoon fish sauce

Remove stems from chiles and place in a mortar. Crush chiles with a pestle to make a paste. Add the garlic and palm sugar and grind the mixture well. Stir in the lime juice, fish sauce, and a drop or two of water if it looks too thick, then pour the mixture into a small serving bowl to serve alongside grilled steak or fish, or just about any other grilled food.

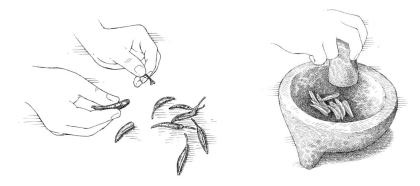

ROMAINE LETTUCE

Second only to iceberg in crispness, but with loads more character, beautiful elongated heads of romaine lettuce in red and green are at their farmers' market peak in summer, and what would the salad world be without them? You can't, for one, toss a proper Caesar without romaine. Another thing you can't make: a romaine dinghy. That's the name the ladies at Brooklyn sandwich shop Saltie have given this oddly satisfying concoction that puts the lettuce leaf center stage. It's like a BLT but without the B or the T, and, amazingly, the dinghy thingy doesn't lack for either.

Saltie's Romaine Dinghy

1 sandwich-size square of focaccia (or *pizza bianca*)

2 tablespoons mayonnaise

4 to 6 large romaine leaves

1 breakfast radish, sliced thin on a mandoline

1 teaspoon chopped anchovy

1 teaspoon minced chive

Juice of half a lemon

Extra-virgin olive oil

Sea salt

Split the bread in half and spread both sides with mayonnaise. Stack romaine leaves and slice crosswise into 3 sections. Toss in a large bowl with the radish, anchovy, chive, lemon juice, olive oil, and sea salt. Stack romaine neatly onto bread, layering each piece with radish and anchovy. *Makes 1 sandwich.*

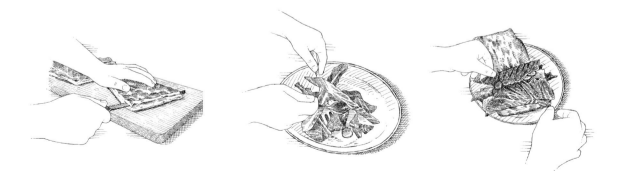

ROMANO BEANS

The broad, flat, edible-pod Romano bean is also known as an Italian green bean, and as such, it's often subjected to the thorough cooking Italians favor when it comes to vegetables, a realm where al dente rarely applies. Ever the traditionalist, Hearth's Marco Canora slow-braises his farmers' market specimens into soft, succulent submission. In this, Canora emphasizes, as in all things, patience is a virtue. And if you've never hand-crushed a ripe tomato before, you're in for a treat.

Marco Canora's Braised Romano Beans

1½ pounds Romano beans

1 large red onion

2 stalks of celery

1 carrot

¼ cup extra-virgin olive oil

5 hand-crushed Roma tomatoes or 1 (12-ounce) can crushed tomatoes

Salt and freshly ground black pepper to taste

⅓ cup chopped basil

Trim stem end of beans and cut larger ones in half. Set aside. Finely chop the onion, celery, and carrot, and sauté them in olive oil with tomatoes for about 20 minutes, until the *soffrito*, or sautéed vegetable mixture, turns pale gold. Add the Romano beans gradually and stir to coat well. Cover and cook over low heat, adding a couple of tablespoons of water if the mixture appears too dry. Cook for about 40 minutes, or until very soft but not falling apart. Season with salt and pepper, and finish with chopped basil. **Serves 4.**

SQUASH BLOSSOMS

*I*n nature, squash blossoms are delicate, ethereal things with a subtle flavor and gorgeous hue. On the plate, they're usually coated in crunchy batter and deep-fried. At midtown Manhattan's wood-fired Beacon, Waldy Malouf has on occasion created an entire menu around them, concluding with this offbeat dessert. Don't worry: whatever health benefit is gained in the baking is lost in the chocolate-crumb coating.

Waldy Malouf's Baked Squash Blossoms with Ricotta and Honey

1½ pounds good-quality fresh ricotta cheese

½ cup honey

1 egg white

18 squash blossoms (12 if they're enormous)

1 egg, beaten with a tablespoon of water

2 cups dry chocolate-cake crumbs or cookie crumbs

Butter, for greasing baking sheet

Preheat oven to 350 degrees. Combine cheese, honey, and egg white. Using a pastry tube or a teaspoon, stuff the squash blossoms about half-full with the cheese mixture. Brush each blossom with the egg wash. Roll each blossom in the cake crumbs and place on a buttered baking sheet. Bake for 12 to 15 minutes, until warm, lightly browned, and crisp. *Serves 6.*

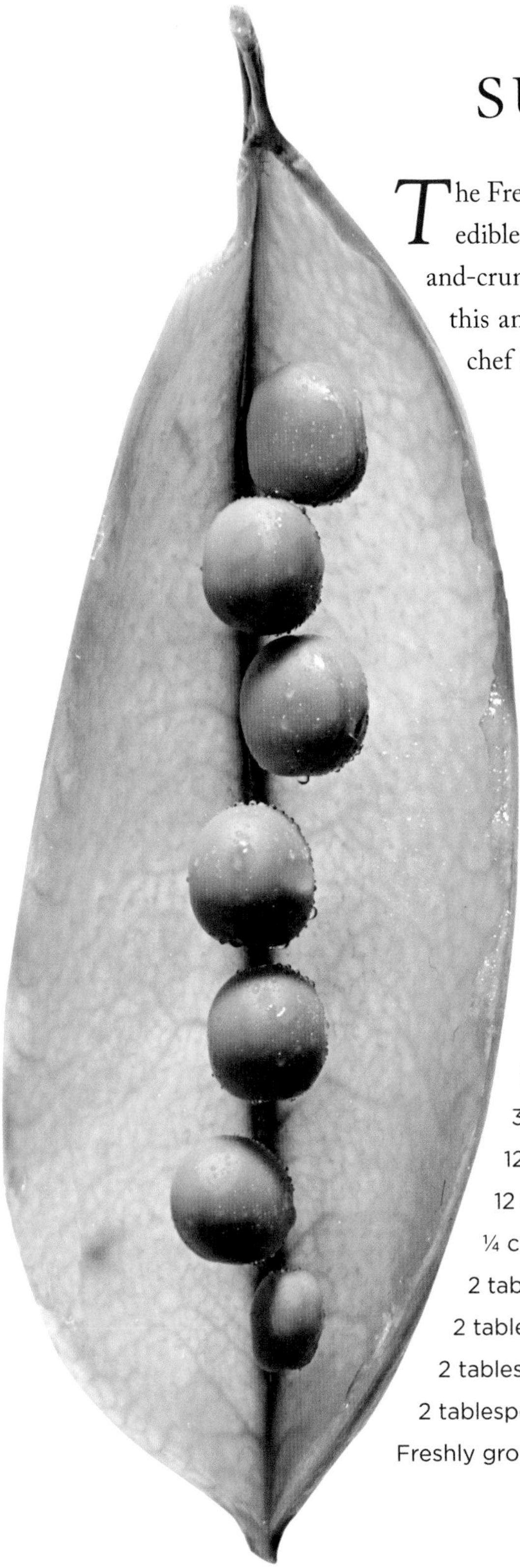

SUGAR SNAP PEAS

The French call them *mange-touts*, or "eat all," referring to the fact that the edible-podded sugar snap is a decidedly nose-to-tail legume, a sweet-and-crunchy package deal. Something else you'll want to eat in its entirety: this amazing snap pea and endive salad from Dan Kluger, the executive chef of Jean-Georges Vongerichten's ABC Kitchen.

Dan Kluger's Sugar Snap Pea and Endive Salad

FOR THE DRESSING

1 cup grated Parmesan cheese

½ cup plus 1 teaspoon Champagne vinegar

¼ cup fresh lime juice

1½ tablespoons Dijon mustard

1 tablespoon kosher salt

1 teaspoon freshly ground black pepper

1 cup sunflower oil

½ cup extra-virgin olive oil

FOR THE SALAD

3 cups sugar snap peas

12 spears Belgian endive

12 spears red endive or radicchio di Treviso

¼ cup Parmesan cheese, grated

2 tablespoons finely chopped parsley

2 tablespoons finely chopped chives

2 tablespoons finely chopped chervil

2 tablespoons finely chopped tarragon

Freshly ground black pepper to taste

FOR THE DRESSING: Combine the Parmesan, vinegar, lime juice, mustard, salt, and pepper in a blender. Emulsify with the oils. Reserve.

FOR THE SALAD: String the snap peas. Bring a pot of water to a boil and blanch the snap peas for 30 seconds. Dry the snap peas, and slice lengthwise into thin strips.

TO PLATE EACH SERVING: Place 1 Belgian- and 1 red-endive spear on a plate. Top with a small mound of sliced snap peas, a drizzle of dressing, and a sprinkle of cheese. Repeat twice, using smaller endives each time. Sprinkle with herbs, and drizzle more dressing around the plate. (Save remaining dressing for another use.) Finish with black pepper. *Serves 4.*

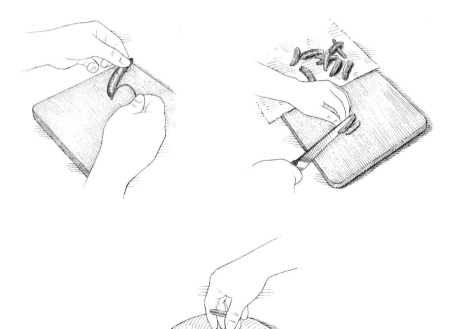

LOCAL ARTICHOKES

With its cool, foggy climate, California might have the domestic-artichoke market cornered. Even so, it's not inconceivable that a small, unheralded local crop could make its way to your neighborhood farmers' market—Manhattan's Greenmarket included. "They love our soil," says Orange County, New York, farmer Jeff Bialas, who tends to a few thousand plants that produce impressive green-petaled globe artichokes beginning in July and continuing right up until the first frost. "They're really very prolific, they just keep comin' on," he says. Try them braised Roman style, fried Roman-Jewish style, or steamed and grilled Bialas style. Or simply slice them raw and toss with lemon, olive oil, and a heroic amount of Parmigiano-Reggiano, as in this recipe from Buvette chef-owner Jody Williams—a California expat but an equal-opportunity artichoke lover.

Jody Williams's Raw Artichoke Salad

3 large lemons (1 for lemon-water bath,
   juice of 2 for salad dressing)
8 medium artichokes
½ cup extra-virgin olive oil

Sea salt and freshly ground black pepper
   to taste
2 cups shaved Parmigiano-Reggiano
   cheese

Prepare a lemon-water bath by squeezing the juice of 1 lemon into a bowl of cold water and tossing in the peels. Through each stage of cleaning and trimming, return the artichokes to the bath to prevent them from browning. (Alternatively, rub the trimmed artichokes with a halved lemon; Williams does both.) Discard the tough, dark-green outer leaves of each artichoke by bending them back and snapping them off, until you reach the pale-yellow inner leaves. With a vegetable peeler, peel the stem and remove the fibrous green base around the bottom of the artichoke. After all of the artichokes have been peeled, slice about an inch off the tops. Slice artichokes in half lengthwise, and remove any sign of a fuzzy choke with a small spoon. Thinly slice artichokes lengthwise and dress generously with olive oil, fresh lemon juice, salt and pepper, and cheese. ***Serves 4.***

AVOCADO SQUASH

*I*f summer comes with a guarantee, it's this: zucchini and its globular, elongated, and crookneck ilk will flood the market, meaning there can never be too many summer squash recipes. Here, one from Txikito's Iberian-inspired co-chef Alex Raij, who stuffs and bakes a Korean variety called Early Bulam that she buys from New Jersey farmer Nevia No, who, for the benefit of her American clientele, sells the vegetable as "avocado squash." The resemblance is uncanny.

Alex Raij's Stuffed Avocado Squash

5 avocado squashes (choose ones that are small and heavy for their size)

¼ cup olive oil, plus more for drizzling

Kosher salt

2 medium leeks, finely chopped

1 small yellow onion, minced

2 tablespoons roughly chopped fresh marjoram leaves

1 bunch scallions, finely sliced

2 hard-boiled eggs, chopped

1½ cups panko bread crumbs

Preheat oven to 475 degrees. Line a baking sheet with parchment paper. Trim a ¾-inch slice off the end of three of the squashes by cutting straight down, and reserve the trim. Slice trimmed squash in half straight through their centers, and place them on the baking sheet face up. Drizzle generously with olive oil and season with salt. Bake for 25 to 35 minutes, until tender but not collapsing. Remove from oven and let rest 5 minutes, then scoop out centers, leaving a border of between ¼ and ½ inch around the edges. Reserve pulp. Chop remaining 2 squashes in chunks, and pulse 6 to 8 times in a food processor with the reserved ends, until the pieces are fine and uniform. In a large sauté pan, heat ¼ cup olive oil. Over low heat, sweat the leeks and onion with salt to taste until translucent. Add marjoram and squash bits and adjust seasoning. Cook until very tender and sweet. Add scallions and fold in reserved pulp. Adjust seasoning. Transfer the mixture to a bowl, and let cool 5 minutes. Fold in chopped egg and panko without overmixing. Loosely mound the stuffing in the squash cups to an inch over the top. (The preceding steps can be done a day ahead and the squash refrigerated.) To serve, reheat in the oven until golden and hot throughout. *Serves 6.*

BREAKFAST RADISHES

*F*or anyone who thinks radishes only come red and round, a trip to a farmers' market is a root-vegetable revelation. The familiar globe variety is joined by long white icicles, psychedelic watermelons, and the elegantly tapered, white-tipped French breakfast—the Coco Chanel of the radish family. The level of spiciness varies, but the crunch is a constant, and that texture is what makes radishes such excellent hors d'oeuvre. Jody Williams, of the West Village's charming Buvette, recommends serving them before dinner with a minimalist take on *bagna cauda*—the "hot bath" of oil, anchovies, and garlic you'll sop up with every last crumb of crusty bread.

Jody Williams's
Breakfast Radishes with Bagna Cauda

12 small to medium radishes (any combination
    of breakfast, icicle, and globe)
Maldon sea salt to taste
½ cup extra-virgin olive oil
5 or so anchovies
2 garlic cloves, crushed

Wash radishes. If some aren't bite-size, cut them in half, and sprinkle with Maldon sea salt. In a small saucepot, gently heat the olive oil (on lowest flame) with the anchovies and the crushed garlic, but don't let the oil begin to bubble. After about 5 minutes, gently stir the anchovies until they disintegrate into a kind of sludgy paste. Remove pot from stove. Distribute the radishes into small serving bowls and drench them with the *bagna cauda*. **Serves 4.**

Clockwise from left: Thai basil, purple basil, sweet basil, bush or Greek basil,
fino verde *basil, lemon basil*

BASIL

Sweet and fragrant basil is at its peak in summer, when it can be found in bountiful bunches wherever herbs are grown. The varieties are seemingly limitless, from the tiny-leaved *fino verde* (good for pesto) to the unbelievably citrusy lemon (try it in soups and salads). The Thai variety may be the most piquant of all, and the one to use in this chicken-basil recipe from the legendary Queens Thai restaurant Sripraphai.

Sripraphai's Pad Kra Pao

2 tablespoons corn oil

6 garlic cloves

15 to 20 Thai or bird chiles, stemmed

1½ pounds ground chicken

2 tablespoons *nam pla* (fish sauce)

2 tablespoons "Thai-style" black salty
    soy sauce

2 tablespoons Golden Mountain
    sauce

1 teaspoon sugar

½ cup fresh Thai basil leaves

2 to 3 slices long hot pepper

Heat the oil in a large pan over medium-high heat. Chop garlic and chiles and add to pan. Sauté for about 30 seconds. Add chicken, *nam pla*, soy sauce, Golden Mountain sauce, and sugar, stirring and chopping up the chicken until fully cooked. Add basil leaves and long hot pepper slices, and cook for just a few more seconds. Serve immediately with rice. ***Serves 4.***

BELL PEPPERS

Overlooked and underrated, the sweet and mild bell pepper is a bit like the farmers' market version of the last kid to be picked for the kickball team. Among all those sleek and fiery horn-shaped chiles you find crowding the bins in August, they don't stand a chance. Still, there's more to do to a bell pepper than stuff it. Grilling or roasting brings out the humble fruit's hidden depths. And dicing and then mingling with farro and Parmigiano-Reggiano, as in Cesare Casella's alt-risotto, is also a very nice way to go. Native Tuscan Casella offers some shopping advice: choose peppers that have smooth, shiny, wrinkle-free skins and some heft and body. Another tip: red, orange, and yellow peppers are riper and sweeter than the green, brown, purple, and white ones. Also: People who say they don't like bell peppers, according to Alice Waters, are simply people who haven't tasted a fully ripe one.

Cesare Casella's Farrotto con Peperoni

2 medium bell peppers, diced

7 cups vegetable stock

2 tablespoons extra-virgin olive oil

1 garlic clove, crushed

1 dried or oil-marinated Calabrian chile

½ small red onion, chopped

1 cup pearled farro

Salt and freshly ground black pepper to taste

¼ cup grated Parmigiano-Reggiano cheese

2 tablespoons chopped parsley

½ cup julienned radicchio

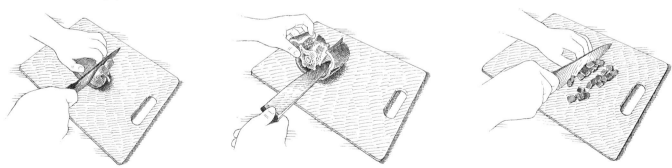

Trim the ends of the peppers. Cut out the core and seeds, and remove any remaining ribs. Dice and reserve. Heat the vegetable stock in a saucepan, and keep hot over low-medium flame. Heat the olive oil in a large sauté pan. Add the garlic and the chile and cook until lightly toasted. Add the onions, and sweat until slightly soft. Stir in the farro, and cook until the grains are coated with oil and toasted. Add about 2½ cups of stock to the farro, and simmer for 15 minutes, stirring occasionally. Add half the remaining stock, and simmer for 10 minutes. Add the rest of the stock, simmer, and stir occasionally, until most of the liquid has been absorbed. Remove the chile and the garlic. Add the diced bell peppers. Season with salt and pepper. Remove pan from heat and stir in the cheese, parsley, and radicchio. *Serves 4 to 6.*

CHERRIES

Sour cherries are compulsory for pie, but sweet ones like Bing and Rainier do well poached, especially in the company of classic companions like port and balsamic vinegar. New York–based pastry chef Pichet Ong appreciates that traditional preparation but also likes to add an Asian twist, as he's been known to do in the kitchens of Spice Market and 66.

Pichet Ong's Sake-Poached Cherries

2 pounds cherries

2 tablespoons sugar

½ vanilla bean, split in half lengthwise and
    seeds scraped (or 1 teaspoon vanilla extract)

¼ cup sweet sake (Ong recommends Komekome)

1 tablespoon rice wine vinegar

¼ teaspoon freshly ground black pepper

¾ cup ricotta cheese

½ teaspoon Maldon sea salt

Stem and pit cherries. Combine cherries, sugar, vanilla bean, and sake in a pot. Simmer for about 5 minutes. Remove from heat. Add vinegar and pepper, cover the pot, and refrigerate for 4 hours. When chilled, divide cherries and accumulated juices among 6 glasses. Top each serving with a spoonful of ricotta, sprinkle a pinch of salt over the cheese, and serve immediately. *Serves 6.*

CORN

Nothing says summer like farmstands piled high with freshly picked corn. If it weren't so agreeably abundant—to paraphrase the late Craig Claiborne—it might enjoy the food-snob appeal of foie gras and truffles. It's hard to beat simply boiled and served with butter, or with its silk removed but its husks pulled back over and tossed on the grill. One of our favorite preparations, though, is this take on the Mexican street snack *esquites* from David Schuttenberg, who ran the kitchen at Zak Pelaccio's terrific but short-lived restaurant Cabrito.

David Schuttenberg's Esquites

4 ears of corn, husks removed

4 tablespoons butter

1 medium white onion, finely chopped

2 garlic cloves, minced

1 stalk *epazote*, stems separated from leaves,
 and leaves finely chopped (see Note)

1 lime, halved

Salt to taste

2 tablespoons Cotija cheese

Chile powder to taste

Note: *The pungent Mexican herb* epazote *can be found fresh at some farmers' market stands or Mexican groceries. If you can't find it, substitute chopped cilantro leaves.*

Over a hot grill or an open gas-stove flame, char 2 ears of corn until well blackened but not completely burnt. Remove from heat, and when cool enough to handle, shave off kernels using a chef's knife and reserve. Remove kernels from remaining 2 ears of corn. Heat a large sauté pan over medium heat. Melt the butter, then add onion and garlic. Sweat for 2 minutes. Add raw corn kernels and stems from the *epazote*, and sauté until corn is just cooked through, about 5 to 7 minutes. Turn heat to high, add the charred kernels of corn to the mixture, and toss to combine until heated through. Squeeze the lime into the mixture. Season with salt. Remove *epazote* stems and spoon mixture into 4 bowls. Top each portion with the Cotija cheese, a pinch of chili powder, and the chopped *epazote* leaves. **Serves 4.**

WILD BLUEBERRIES

Smaller, glossier, and richer in flavor than their cultivated brethren, wild blueberries are a glorious thing. And so, it hardly needs saying, is blueberry pie. The rendition pastry chef Emily Isaac created for Union Square Cafe before decamping to open her own Brooklyn pastry shop, Trois Pommes Patisserie, is endearingly homey—not quite as sweet as August in Maine, but almost.

Emily Isaac's Blueberry Pie

FOR THE CRUST

2 ⅔ sticks of butter, cut into ½-inch cubes and frozen

2 ⅔ cups all-purpose flour

Pinch of salt

4 tablespoons ice water

FOR THE FILLING

6 cups wild blueberries

1 cup sugar plus 1 tablespoon

Zest and juice of 1 large lemon

3 tablespoons cornstarch

Pinch of salt

1 egg, beaten with 1 teaspoon water

FOR THE CRUST: Combine butter, flour, and salt in food processor and blend until butter is pea-size. With blade turning, add water, one tablespoon at a time, until the dough holds together. Divide dough into two equal disks, wrap in plastic, and allow to rest in refrigerator for 1 hour. Remove one disk and roll out on a lightly floured surface to about 12 inches in diameter. Place the dough in a 10-inch pie pan and press it down to conform to shape of pan. Trim any excess dough from edges. Cover with plastic wrap and set pan aside in refrigerator.

FOR THE PIE: Place oven rack in middle position and preheat to 325 degrees. Rinse berries and place them in a pot with ½ cup of the sugar. Cook over medium heat for about 3 to 4 minutes, stirring occasionally, until their juice begins to flow. Remove the pot from heat, strain berries in a colander set over a bowl, and allow to cool. Transfer berries to a bowl and toss in the remaining ½ cup sugar, lemon zest and juice, cornstarch, and salt. Allow to macerate for ten minutes. Roll out the remaining disk of dough to a 12-inch circle and set aside. Remove pie shell from refrigerator and spoon the fruit mixture into the shell. Place the disk of dough on top of the fruit filling and seal the rim by pressing down gently around the edges of the pan. Trim the excess dough with a knife and crimp the edge with fingers or a fork. Brush the top with egg wash and sprinkle with the remaining sugar. Cut 5 slits into the top of the pie to allow steam to escape. Bake for 45 minutes, until the crust is golden brown and filling is bubbling. Allow to cool before serving. *Serves 8.*

SUN GOLD TOMATOES

Although late summer is all about the heirlooms, not all hybrids are inherently inferior. Take the incredibly sweet Sun Gold variety, for example. No less a member of the tomato cognoscenti than Mario Batali is a big fan. At Babbo, he tosses them by the wagonload with garlic and lemon basil into a thicket of *bavette,* the long, dried pasta from Genoa. It's a cinch to prepare—the only real skill required is a firm resolve not to pop all those delicious cherry tomatoes into your mouth before the pan heats up.

Babbo's Bavette *with Sun Gold Tomatoes*

2 tablespoons salt, for pasta

¼ cup extra-virgin olive oil

4 garlic cloves, thinly sliced

2 pints Sun Gold cherry tomatoes, whole

½ bunch chives, cut into 1-inch lengths

12 fresh lemon basil leaves, finely shredded

Salt and freshly ground black pepper to taste

1 pound *bavette* (or linguine or spaghetti)

Bring a large pot of water to a boil, and add salt. In a 12- to 14-inch sauté pan, heat the olive oil over high heat until almost smoking. Lower the heat to medium high and add the garlic. Cook for 2 minutes or until softened and slightly browned. Add the tomatoes, chives, and basil, and cook over high heat until the tomatoes are just beginning to burst. Season with salt and pepper. Meanwhile, add the pasta to the boiling water and cook until al dente. Drain pasta and add it to the pan with the tomatoes. Toss over high heat for 1 minute, then divide among four warmed pasta bowls and serve immediately. *Serves 4.*

TOMATILLOS

Although it's a member of the same nightshade family as tomatoes, the tart, lemony tomatillo, or Mexican green tomato, is used when it's green and firm rather than ripe and juicy. Like the cape gooseberry, to which it's also related, the fruit is wrapped in a dry, papery husk harboring a sticky substance that needs to be scrubbed off before cooking—but with just a quick chop and a whir in the blender, we're not entirely sure Sueños chef Sue Torres's super-simple salsa recipe really constitutes cooking. There is absolutely no doubt, though, that the vibrant green purée tastes infinitely better than anything you'll find on a supermarket shelf.

Sue Torres's Tomatillo Salsa

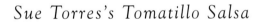

10 large or 12 medium tomatillos

3 serrano chiles

½ cup white onion, minced, plus an
   additional ¼ cup

½ garlic clove, minced

¼ cup roughly chopped cilantro

Kosher salt

Husk and wash the tomatillos well. Stem and chop them and the chiles. In a blender or food processor, purée the tomatillos, chiles, ½ cup minced onion, garlic, and cilantro until mixture is smooth. Pour into a large serving bowl, season to taste with kosher salt, and stir in the remaining ¼ cup of minced onion for texture. Serve immediately, or refrigerate for 24 hours so that the flavors can marry.

SWEET POTATO LEAVES

Vegetable completists who devour every edible part of the plant, from beet green to garlic scape, will relish the sweet-potato leaf, a late-summer harbinger of the iconic Thanksgiving tuber. Although widely consumed in West Africa, Malaysia, and the Philippines, the heart-shaped leaves are rarer in the United States. But now that an increasing number of farmers have been bringing them to market, you might be seeing more of the mild-flavored leaves on restaurant menus. Blanched and simply seasoned, they make a fine addition to Takashi chef-owner Takashi Inoue's *namul* plate of assorted vegetables.

Takashi Inoue's Namul of Sweet Potato Leaves

1 bunch sweet potato leaves

1 teaspoon salt

1 tablespoon sesame oil

1 teaspoon sesame seeds

1 teaspoon minced garlic

Remove stems from sweet potato leaves. Peel off the skin with your fingers, then cut stems into 1-inch strands. In a large saucepan filled with boiling water, blanch the leaves for 10 seconds, then the stems for 45 seconds, and drain well. In a bowl, combine salt, sesame oil, sesame seeds, and minced garlic, and mix well. Add the sweet potato leaves and stems, and toss. Serve immediately or let rest up to 3 hours. *Serves 4 as an appetizer.*

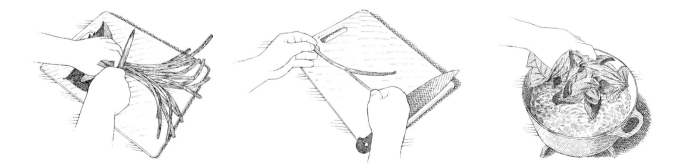

TURKISH ORANGE EGGPLANT

No, what you're looking at is not a miniature pumpkin but rather a full-grown Turkish orange eggplant, a two-inch heirloom variety, available at some farmers' markets in late summer. The little guys are almost too cute to eat, but don't let that stop you. Slice them paper thin on a mandoline and fry them in oil to make eggplant chips. Or even better, dredge them in cornmeal the way they do green tomatoes down South, and call them fried orange eggplants.

Fried Orange Eggplants

12 Turkish orange eggplants

Vegetable oil, for frying

¾ cup cornmeal

1 tablespoon salt

1 teaspoon freshly ground black pepper

½ cup milk

2 eggs

Cut the eggplants into ½-inch slices, discarding ends. In a large skillet, add oil to a depth of approximately ⅓ inch and heat over medium heat until very hot. In a large shallow bowl, combine the cornmeal, salt, and pepper. In another bowl, whisk together the milk and eggs. Working in batches, dredge eggplant slices in seasoned cornmeal, dip in egg wash, then dredge once more in cornmeal. Add as many slices to the hot oil as will fit without crowding the pan and cook on each side until golden brown. *Serves 4 to 6.*

WATERMELON

*I*n the steamy swelter of summer, when the thought of turning on the oven is anathema, there are few things more refreshing than sweet, juicy watermelon and cool, crunchy cucumber—two plants that happen to belong to the same botanical family. Johan Svensson, formerly of New York's Aquavit and currently the chef of BLT Steak in Waikiki, combines them in an ingenious cold chile-spiked soup that gets even colder with the addition of ice cubes made from the soup itself.

Johan Svensson's Chilled Watermelon and Cucumber Soup

1 small seedless watermelon (large enough to yield a pound of fruit)

2 seedless cucumbers, peeled and chopped into 1-inch pieces

1 *piri-piri* chile, minced (remove seeds for a less spicy soup)

½ garlic clove, minced

Juice of half a lemon

2 tablespoons olive oil

Salt and freshly ground white pepper to taste

Cut watermelon into large chunks and remove rind. In a high-speed mixer, blender, or food processor, combine all ingredients except salt and pepper, and blend until smooth. Season to taste. Fill one ice-cube tray with soup and freeze for at least 4 hours. Chill remaining soup in fridge. When ready to serve, ladle into 4 bowls and add the frozen cubes. If desired, garnish with a slice of grilled melon or shrimp seviche. *Serves 4.*

WILD ALASKAN KING SALMON

Among the five varieties of wild Pacific salmon, the silver-backed king (aka chinook) from cold Alaskan waters is the most highly prized. (The red-fleshed sockeye is a close second.) Its flesh is firm and comparatively fatty, with a rich, complex flavor that evokes the sea and puts the farmed stuff to shame. Thanks to well-managed, sustainable fishing practices, wild Alaskan salmon habitats are in good shape, so you needn't feel a pang of guilt as you tuck into a nice fillet. The season varies according to river and geography, but generally speaking, it runs from early summer and into the fall. Cooking a fish of this caliber, like cooking a USDA prime steak, should be an exercise in restraint. At upward of $30 a pound, you don't want to muck it up. Simply pan-frying the way Dave Pasternack does at his Manhattan seafood shrine Esca is the way to go. A tip from the master: to get the skin crisp, press down on the fillets with your hand while cooking.

Dave Pasternack's Alaskan King Salmon with Sugar Snap Peas

¾ pound sugar snap peas

5 tablespoons canola oil

4 (8-ounce) wild king salmon fillets

Salt and pepper to taste

¼ cup extra-virgin olive oil, plus more for finishing

1 ounce *guanciale* or pancetta, julienned

⅓ cup black mint leaves

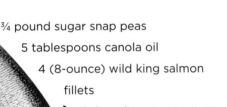

Bring a large pot of salted water to a boil. Add the sugar snap peas and cook for 2 minutes. Remove and place in ice water to stop the cooking. In a nonstick sauté pan, heat the canola oil until hot but not smoking. Add the fillets skin side down and lower the flame. Cook the salmon for approximately 5 minutes or until the desired level of doneness is reached. Season to taste. In another pan, heat the olive oil with the *guanciale*. Render *guanciale* until golden but not crispy. Add the sugar snap peas and 2 tablespoons of water. Heat through, add mint, and remove from the heat. Plate each fillet of salmon with a portion of the sugar snap peas. Drizzle with olive oil and serve. ***Serves 4.***

ZUCCHINI

In its endlessly prolific bounty, zucchini can often seem more like a curse than a blessing. But all you need is one great recipe, like this one from Franny's, to feel entirely different about the thin-skinned summer squash. Even this most innocuous of vegetables—well, fruits, technically—has no choice but to shine in the face of a shallow fry, a garlicky marinade, and a vibrant herb garnish.

Franny's Marinated Zucchini with Mint and Scallions

2 pounds zucchini (about 4 green and 4 yellow), trimmed

Kosher salt

2 cups thinly sliced scallions

1 cup extra-virgin olive oil

½ cup red wine vinegar

¼ cup sliced garlic

Crushed red pepper flakes, to taste

Freshly ground black pepper

1 bunch mint, stemmed and washed

1 bunch basil, stemmed and washed

Slice zucchini into ½-inch-thick rounds. Salt generously and put in a colander over a bowl. Place the sliced scallions in cold water. Refrigerate both for 1 hour. Remove zucchini and dry thoroughly. Heat the oil in a heavy-bottomed sauté pan over a medium-high flame. Fry zucchini in small batches until golden brown, roughly 3 to 4 minutes per side. Place browned slices on a large serving platter; when all the zucchini has been cooked, sprinkle slices with red wine vinegar. Lower the heat and add the garlic to the remaining oil left in the pan, stirring and turning frequently enough to infuse the oil but not brown the garlic (this should be quick). Remove pan from heat, and add the red pepper flakes and a few grinds of pepper. Pour the oil over the fried zucchini and let it sit at least 30 minutes. Rinse and spin-dry the scallions. Combine them in a bowl with the mint and basil, season with salt and pepper, and add a few spoonfuls of the zucchini marinade. Top the zucchini with the herbs and serve. *Serves 6*.

ACKNOWLEDGMENTS

For anyone who eats or cooks in New York, very little has made more of an impact on our menus or plates over the last three-plus decades than Greenmarket and its participating network of farmers and producers. Without them—and the program's ever-helpful organizational staff—this book wouldn't be possible.

It's also a direct consequence of the vision of *New York* editor-in-chief Adam Moss, who conceived of a column that could be both beautiful and instructive. Thanks to our editor, Jon Gluck, for seeing the project through with great enthusiasm and care. We are grateful to the team of photographers, photo editors (especially Leonor Mamanna and Jody Quon), and designers who work every week to make it so, and to John Burgoyne, whose illustrations bring written technique to vivid life.

We are lucky to live in one of the world's greatest food capitals, and to be surrounded by chefs who are not only incredibly creative and talented, but also generous. We thank all of them for their inspired contributions.

Thanks also to our colleagues Gillian Duffy, Mary Jane Weedman, and Christine Whitney for testing some of these recipes; and to designer Bianca Jackson for her invaluable help.

We're also extremely grateful to Sarah Hochman, David Rosenthal, and the whole Blue Rider Press team for so seamlessly transforming a magazine column into a cookbook, a monumental job they made look easy.

ILLUSTRATION AND PHOTO CREDITS

Cover photography by Kenneth Chen, Danny Kim, Kang Kim, Richard Pierce, Carina Salvi, Kenji Toma, Hannah Whitaker.

Line drawings throughout by John Burgoyne.

Kenneth Chen: pages 18, 52, 73, 84, 98, 101

Davies & Starr: pages 94, 145

Keith Douglas/Alamy: page 205

Henry Hargreaves: page 198

Danny Kim: pages iv (Bosc Pears), 1 (Kohlrabi, Bosc Pears), 5, 6, 8, 10, 19, 25, 26, 42, 44, 45, 46, 57, 59 (Rutabaga), 67, 71, 72, 80, 85, 87, 97, 104, 122, 139, 141, 147, 148, 153, 164, 175, 178, 202, 203

Kang Kim: pages iv (Sun Gold Tomatoes), 1 (Escarole, Pomegranates), 2, 15, 20, 21, 24, 29, 37, 39, 40, 41, 49, 51, 55, 59 (Crawfish), 60, 64, 70, 77, 78, 82, 89, 90, 92, 99, 100, 106, 107, 108, 109, 111 (Eggs), 119, 120, 126, 131, 133, 137, 150, 151, 152, 156, 159 (Kirby Cucumbers, Santa Rosa Plums, Purple Eggplant), 161, 162, 163, 165, 166, 168, 169, 171, 172, 176, 179, 181, 184, 185, 188, 190, 192, 200, 201, 206

Ocean/Corbis: pages 159 (Cherries), 196

Boru O'Brien O'Connell: page 195

Richard Pierce: page 53

Carina Salvi: pages iv (Fiddlehead Ferns), 13, 16, 34, 48, 59 (Northern Spy Apples), 62, 68, 69, 76, 88, 91, 111 (Ramps, Soft-Shell Crabs), 112, 114, 115, 116, 117, 118, 123, 124, 130, 136, 143, 144, 173, 182, 191, 204

Kenji Toma: pages 9, 14, 38

Josh Westrich/Zefa/Corbis: page 86

Hannah Whitaker: pages iv (Maine Shrimp), 12, 23, 30, 32, 35, 36, 59 (Maine Shrimp), 63, 74, 96, 103, 105, 111 (Pineapple), 121, 128, 135, 138, 154, 183, 186, 197

INDEX

ABOUT THE AUTHORS

Rob Patronite and Robin Raisfeld edit the weekly food coverage in *New York* magazine's "Strategist" section and write monthly restaurant reviews as well as special features on food and dining. Their annual "Eat Cheap" guide is one of the magazine's bestselling issues and their weekly "In Season" column has been anthologized in *The Best American Recipes 2005–2006: The Year's Top Picks from Books, Magazines, Newspapers, and the Internet.* They have twice won National Magazine Awards, and have been nominated for three James Beard Awards.